ENGAGING WITH PARENTS IN EARLY YEARS SETTINGS

Education at SAGE

SAGE is a leading international publisher of journals, books, and electronic media for academic, educational, and professional markets.

Our education publishing includes:

- accessible and comprehensive texts for aspiring education professionals and practitioners looking to further their careers through continuing professional development
- inspirational advice and guidance for the classroom
- authoritative state of the art reference from the leading authors in the field.

Find out more at: **www.sagepub.co.uk/education**

DIANNE JACKSON AND MARTIN NEEDHAM

ENGAGING WITH PARENTS IN EARLY YEARS SETTINGS

Los Angeles | London | New Delhi
Singapore | Washington DC

SAGE Publications Ltd
1 Oliver's Yard
55 City Road
London EC1Y 1SP

SAGE Publications Inc.
2455 Teller Road
Thousand Oaks, California 91320

SAGE Publications India Pvt Ltd
B 1/I 1 Mohan Cooperative Industrial Area
Mathura RoadA
New Delhi 110 044

SAGE Publications Asia-Pacific Pte Ltd
3 Church Street
#10-04 Samsung Hub
Singapore 049483

© Martin Needham and Dianne Jackson, 2014

First edition published 2014

Library of Congress Control Number: 2013952957

British Library Cataloguing in Publication data

A catalogue record for this book is available from the British Library

ISBN 978-1-4462-5895-8 (p)
ISBN 978-1-4462-5894-1

Editor: Jude Bowen and Amy Jarrold
Associate editor: Miriam Davey
Project manager: Jeanette Graham
Production editor: Nicola Marshall
Copyeditor: Carol Lucas
Proofreader: Nicola Marshall
Indexers: Dianne Jackson and Martin Needham
Marketing executive: Dilhara Attygalle
Cover design: Wendy Scott
Typeset by: Dorwyn, Wells, Somerset
Printed in India by: Replika Press Pvt Ltd

For Liz and Christine with thanks for showing us that nurture, playful cognitive challenge and independent enquiry are important at every stage of learning.

Contents

List of figures

About the authors

Dianne Jackson trained as an Early Childhood Teacher and taught in a broad range of community, early childhood and school settings. Dianne then became a lecturer in the School of Education at the University of Western Sydney where she completed a First Class Honours degree in social science. Since 2004 Dianne has held the position of Chief Executive Officer at Connect Child and Family Services, a non-governmental organisation (NGO) in outer western Sydney that delivers a broad range of early childhood focused programmes with families. Dianne holds an adjunct position at the University of Western Sydney where she completed her PhD in 2010 and her doctoral research won the 2010 European Early Childhood Research Association (EECERA) Best Practitioner Research Award. Dianne co-convenes an EECERA special interest research group and her organisation has recently opened an innovative parent and child meeting place, conceptually based on collaborative work she has done with her EECERA colleagues from the University of Ghent. Dianne is also the New South Wales state convenor for the Australian Research Alliance for Children and Youth (ARACY).

Martin Needham trained and worked as an Early Years Teacher in Nottinghamshire, London and Pakistan. This was followed by four years as an Early Years Development Officer for a local authority working on a range of initiatives including Early Years Development and Childcare Partnerships, and Children's Centres. During this time he worked regularly with one of the regional parent and child groups as part of the National Children's Bureau's Playing with Words project. He became a Senior Lecturer in Early Childhood Studies at the University of Wolverhampton in 2003 and a Principal Lecturer at Manchester Metropolitan University in 2014. Martin completed his PhD *Examining Pedagogy and Learning with Children Under the Age of 4* at the Institute of Education, London University, in 2011. Martin has two children with whom he attended parent and toddler groups. He has published titles on multi-agency working *The Team around the Child* (Siraj-Blatchford et al., 2007) and Applying Theory to Practice (Waller et al., 2011). Martin was the external examiner for the Peers Early Education Partnership (PEEP) which delivers practitioner training for those working with parents and children together from 2006 to 2010. Martin has also conducted research into leadership in early years settings (Hadfield et al., 2012).

References

Hadfield, M., Jopling, M., Needham, M., Waller, T., Coleyshaw, L., Emira, M. and Royle, K. (2012) *Longitudinal Study of Early Years Professional Status: An Exploration of Progress, Leadership and Impact – Final Report*. London: Department for Education.
Siraj-Blatchford, I., Clarke, K. and Needham, M. (2007) *The Team Around the Child: Multi-agency Working in the Early Years*. Stoke-on-Trent: Trentham.
Waller, T., Whitmarsh, J. and Clarke, K. (2011) *The Power of Ideas in the Early Years*. Maidenhead: Open University Press.

Acknowledgements

This book is the culmination of research that we undertook with parents, families and practitioners in dual-focused groups in England and Australia. These people generously shared their time, thoughts and experiences with us and we learned so much from them. It is with the greatest appreciation that we thank them for the considerable contribution their participation has now made to early years service provision and the well-being of children and families.

We would also like to thank the institutions which have supported us both professionally and financially. Martin would especially like to thank his friends and colleagues at the University of Wolverhampton in the School of Education and those at the Institute of Education, London University.

Dianne would like to thank the University of Western Sydney School of Education where she completed her doctoral studies and now holds an adjunct position, and Connect Child and Family Services where she is the Chief Executive Officer. The support and expertise of friends and colleagues in both of these organisations continues to inform and influence her thinking and work.

We would especially like to thank our PhD supervisors Liz Brooker and Christine Woodrow.

We are both also very grateful to the European Early Childhood Education Research Association (EECERA) for providing a regular meeting place as a platform for developing this book. We met as new doctoral students presenting individual papers in a symposium session at an EECERA conference and have worked collaboratively since then.

Finally, but most importantly, we would like to thank our own families whose love and support continues to sustain us; Dianne's partner Arnd and their five children continue to be the inspiration for her work; Martin's partner Ginny and their two children continue to be his best critical friends.

Preface

We have used the term 'parent' throughout this book, however it is extremely important to point out that we take this to be an inclusive term encompassing guardians and grandparents of both sexes. The dual-focused groups used as examples explicitly promoted 'family' involvement but this word sometimes suggests a large number of family members participating at the same time. The word 'parent' in this context gives a more accurate sense of one adult attending group sessions with one, two or more of their children.

The book was written with the intention of assisting and informing those who have an interest in engaging and working alongside parents and children in joint activities and dual-focused groups. We hope to prompt purposeful reflection on key issues for those who support younger children's participation in settings together with their parents.

The book is presented in three parts. Part 1 reviews young children's development, researching with parents and the case for joint activity involving parents, children and practitioners. Part 2 uses examples from dual-focused groups in Australia to discuss what parents experience as support in these settings, the importance of nurture and the critical nature of facilitation in this context. Part 3 examines the nature of the learning environment experienced by children using examples of parent and toddler sessions in England.

Each chapter begins with an overview and presents a key idea. At least one case study example is also included with suggestions for reflective activities that we hope will further extend readers' thinking on the topics in the chapter either individually or collaboratively with others. The sequenced progression of the chapters in the book forms an argument for developing and sustaining joint activities between children, parents and practitioners. Each chapter, however, is also accessible in its own right and can be used to inform particular aspects of early years provision. We also hope that this structure will lend itself both to existing courses and to the more specialised study of promoting with parents.

Foreword

Starting with parents; supporting children in the early years

The discipline of working to achieve more authentically participatory, democratically oriented and research-informed early childhood practice has grown rapidly in recent years and it is now widely accepted as a powerful transformative force in early childhood practice internationally. In our own work we have made visible our continuing struggle to operate authentically within a participatory worldview in the belief that early childhood practice should and could be more democratic, participatory, empowering and should also be deeply ethical and political in its orientation (Pascal and Bertram, 2009, 2012). This shared journey of exploration and discovery still goes on and continues to enchant and beguile us. It is wonderful to see other scholars in the sector rising to the challenge of making this aspiration a reality.

This fascinating and informed book from two well respected scholars from England and Australia, about how we might more effectively work with parents to support their children's learning attempts to achieve such a world view, appears at a significant time for those who work in early childhood services as they undergo a radical process of expansion, transformation and improvement. A major perspective shift has occurred which demands that early childhood services be transformed from being solely child focused to being child and parent focused. It is now increasingly accepted that early childhood practitioners have a professional responsibility, and therefore a professional skill requirement, to work with parents and children together to create a triad of developmental interaction with the child as they grow and thrive. For many in the sector, the system historically has divided those who work with parents from those who work with children. However, this timely book knits this fragmented thinking back together in a clear message that working in collaborative and nurturing child, parent, practitioner contexts has to be the future.

In early childhood there is also a sharper need than ever to bring together theory, research and practice to ensure this change process is the result of careful thought and informed professional knowledge. In this relevant and reflective book, we find a set of chapters which demonstrate the synergy between research, theory and practice in early childhood beautifully. The authors of this book have succeeded in putting reflexivity and praxis at the heart of their work. This book is important because it provides a clear demonstration of the potential energy which is released when theory and practice come together, increasing the impact and complexity of the narratives of practice that result. Each chapter provides a layered narrative of praxis as the authors seek to explain and understand the complexities of working together with parents to support the fantastic and enthralling early learning journey of these very young children. It is both timely and enormously helpful to those in the field who are attempting to establish a new paradigm of work with parents and children.

It is inspiring to see a text which attempts to shift our worldview, to support existing and developing practitioners and researchers to reflect more critically on how to more authentically realize the participatory practice with parents that they strive for. This requires courage, risk taking, and further innovation, alongside a more rigorous and critical engagement in the documentation of practice and a deeper level of reflection on the consequences of their actions. This shift could give us the chance to achieve more open, inclusive, democratic early childhood practice that has the capacity to answer the deeper questions we face in developing a more socially just ECEC system of practice which sees both parents and children as powerful and positive agents in their own futures.

Chris Pascal and Tony Bertram

References 📖

Pascal, C. and Bertram, T. (2009) 'Listening to young citizens: the struggle to make real a participatory paradigm in research with young children', *European Early Childhood Research Journal*, 17 (2): 249–62.

Pascal, C. and Bertram, T. (2009) 'Praxis, Ethics and Power: developing praxeology as a participatory paradigm for early childhood research', *European Early Childhood Research Journal*, 20 (4): 477–92.

PART 1

PARENTS, CHILDREN AND PRACTITIONERS TOGETHER

The nature of human development

Chapter overview

Chapter 1 offers a summary of the factors which we believe are important to bear in mind when seeking to support young children's development. The process of learning shaped by the nature of the human mind and its desire to make sense of the natural and social worlds is outlined. This is followed by a review of the processes that exist within families which interact with, guide and shape, the child's social, emotional and cognitive development. We stress the value of focusing on dispositions towards life and learning compared with the immediate transfer of knowledge from adults to children. In the final part of the chapter we seek to illustrate how relationships and interactions enacted within the context of practitioner-supported parent and child groups offer valuable opportunities for parents, children and practitioners to learn from each other.

Introduction

In this book we explore the role that professionals can play in working with parents to support young children's development and education. We argue that this role needs to be considered in the context of a rapidly changing modern era and with increasing the understanding and expectations of the importance of early childhood. At face value this does not appear to be too controversial, however, since the introduction of the idea of the welfare state following the Second World War, this has proved to be difficult to put into practice and controversial in terms of the relationship between state and the home. We will examine the competing interests and potential barriers to the exchange of knowledge between parents and practitioners in later chapters but we begin by considering the nature of what it is to be human, how humans learn and the role of society and family in facilitating that learning. We concentrate on the way day-to-day experiences shape children, these are in one sense very ordinary, but reflect the extraordinary nature of what it is to be human and how that humanity is passed from one generation to the next.

Children, parents and professionals learning together

Many societies are increasingly coming to an understanding of the importance of early childhood and many are shifting from a view of infants as helpless, empty vessels, who might be swaddled and restrained and who should speak only when spoken to (Maybin and Woodhead, 2003). Instead young children are now being viewed as resilient, active learners, who are eager to explore their world and to engage with others. We see them as hard wired to make sense of the world and eager to participate in activity using play as a tool to develop mastery over skills, ideas and practices on the way to becoming valued members of society.

This shift in attitudes towards children, along with rapidly changing social structures, demands that we reflect on the changing processes and patterns of child-rearing. There is not necessarily a tension between an individual's and society's model of the world, however there is a dynamic between the two. This dynamic is not purely rational and embedded in the logic of the world; it is also influenced by traditions, emotions and preferences. What we accept to be true as individuals, as groups and as societies is evolving over time as we learn more, develop new tools and live in new ways that respond to changing circumstances.

Issues of care, play, discipline and social relationships continue to be renegotiated by each new generation of parents according to the contexts in which they find themselves. With this in mind, this book aims to reflect on key ideas and research processes that enable practitioners to work alongside children and parents together, and to be responsive to changing circumstances. We begin with an account of an interconnected view of development that indicates how attitudes, life and learning might be shaped in relationships with parents and communities.

Human nature

The first decade of a new millennium has seen a flourishing of new scientific tools for the study of human development; brain scanning techniques and genetic sequencing have reopened old debates about our nature and nurture and informed the increasing interest in the ways in which we raise children in our rapidly changing societies (Goswami, 2008). The unravelling of the human genome is also making it increasingly clear that humans are creatures which share much in common, not just with near neighbours such as the great apes, but also with creatures which appear to be very different, such as mice and reptiles. Theories of learning now need to explain how we learn through the mechanisms of perception which have evolved through millennia of ancestors and which continue to shape the way in which we experience the world (Dawkins, 2004).

Darwin (1928) outlines how species of bee and finch are shaped by the way they interact with the environment and suggests that one can tell one species from another, not necessarily by their appearance but by what they do: that is, their phenotype. The revelation of the similarity of our genetics to other creatures, highlights that humanity is remarkable because of its use of complex socialised tools such as language and the everyday systems that form cultures. The idea that humans have evolved and are defined by the nature of what they do is at the centre of Darwin's theory of evolution.

Vygotsky and Piaget studied children's development through their interactions with their environments. This underpins their theories of learning and they are the two most cited influences on the way we now plan support for children's development (Athey, 2007). Piaget (1950) argued that humans are born curious, with a desire to make sense of the world and that the understanding they develop is shaped by the way they process their experiences.

Vygotsky (1986) argued that children's development is shaped and sculpted by the activities that society has to offer. So the activities, tools, words and thoughts that cultures have evolved, shape the minds of each new generation. The study of the interaction between organisms' genetic drivers and their environment is called epigenetics, and it is something that Piaget and Vygotsky were both interested in but studied in slightly different ways.

Pinker (2002) demonstrated that the interplay between environment and genetics is much more sensitive than first thought. Sharot (2012) suggests that actions and environment around the time of conception and through the antenatal period influence not just the physical nature of children at birth, but also their dispositions to development. Just as surprisingly, behaviours throughout the life period can amend and alter the trajectory of physical development. Rogoff (1990) asserts that from birth, children's development occurs in a biologically given social matrix characteristic of our species. Different communities produce variations in the specific genetic and special resources of new individual members, and these variations are as essential to understanding human development as are the genetic and social resources that humans have in common.

This initial chapter considers the holistic way that children's cognitive knowledge develops, driven by their genetic inheritance and shaped by their actions and environment. It highlights the factors that might inform the structure and format of activities and environments which are deliberately structured for parents and children to share together.

The human infant's mind and society

In early education we are increasingly secure in the value of offering children opportunities to explore and make sense of their environment. We regard children under 3 as active participants in developing their own learning rather than passively evolving organisms. Piaget (1950) argued that development was epigenetic, suggesting that the mind was pro-grammed to develop in certain ways and that it was necessary to engage with experiences to realise potential.

Modern research affirms Piaget's constructivist perspective and suggests that knowledge is formed through the interplay between genetic meaning-making and pattern-seeking, programming the brain with experience. The brain may be much more flexible then was thought previously and may be constructed to function in different ways by the environments and tools to which humans adapt. We now know that the first three years of life see the activation of tremendous networks of connections between the neurones in children's brains. This happens in unique patterns through interaction with the sights, smells, tastes, feelings and thoughts that they encounter (Mareschal, et al. 2004).

Children's everyday experiences are absorbed holistically and patterns of similar sensory experience gradually become associated and linked through the formation of dendritic connections in the brain. These patterns of connection in turn filter future events in unique ways to the individual. The sensorimotor period, associated with Piaget (1950) occurs during the first two years and continues to be characterised by children investigating their world through each of their senses and through patterns of movement. These then form their frameworks for referencing and understanding the world.

What neuroscience investigations have also revealed is the rapid development of connections between neurones in the brain. This development peaks in early childhood and is followed by the reduction or pruning of less used synapses and the strengthening of frequently used pathways beyond the age of 5 towards adulthood (Goswami, 2008). One suggestion for this phenomenon is that the familiarity of particular experiences channel and strengthen particular patterns in the brain and that rarely used connections dissipate. It is also hypothesised that the development of language and other shared cultural tools may also help to structure ideas into groups and thus assist this process of shaping the workings of the mind.

Such a view lends support for the increasing role of culture in shaping our thinking in particular ways. It is this sociocultural dimension which Vygotsky and his colleagues, Luria and Leont'ev (Leont'ev, 1978) identi-fied when they realised that humans raised in similar literate environments came to think using similar tools and in ways which were significantly different to those raised in isolated rural communities with no schooling or literacy (Leont'ev, 1978). They suggested that the reason that we are able to communicate is that our general physical and emotional needs are similar and that for much of human history the tools we have used are similar.

Thus children construct their mental models of the world in a very social context. One in which they are guided by their introduction into participation in social activities. Most languages have evolved similar ideas and have equivalent words. Children follow similar patterns of becoming walking, talking, social beings because their genetic growth is similar and because they are raised in social communities that have developed over the last 20 millennia.

🔑 Key idea: an ecological perspective

Bronfenbrenner's ecological perspective of human development provides a foundation for the investigation of relationships between children, parents and professionals. This perspective forms a central framework for linking the ideas in this book together, so is helpful to begin with a consideration of Bronfenbrenner's view of children's development.

Bronfenbrenner (1979) saw children's development as being influenced by a complex system of interconnected relationships. He emphasised the dynamic nature of the interactions between children and their environments and acknowledged the many influences on development that arise from a diverse range of relationships. This is one of the strengths of the ecological model.

(Continues)

(Continued)

The ecological model includes five systems that range from direct interactions between people to broad contexts of culture. These systems are known as microsystems, ecosystems, exosystems, macrosystems and chrono-systems. Any relationships which occur between children and their immediate environments are referred to as microsystems and include families and peers. Mesosystems result from the interrelationships between two or more microsystems that children participate in, for example, the inter-relationship between home (one microsystem) and parent/child groups (another microsystem).

Settings that affect children but that they are not directly involved in, such as parents' workplaces, are known as exosystems. The macrosystems within the model refer to beliefs and attitudes within the cultures in which children live and the chronosystem refers to patterns of environmental events and transitions that influence the life course.

Recommended further reading

Bronfenbrenner, H. (1979) *The Ecology of Human Development*. Cambridge, MA: Harvard University Press.

This book focuses on the interrelationship between two mesosystems: children's homes and dual-focused groups. It highlights the ability of these interrelationships to engender what Bronfenbrenner describes as molar change, that is, lasting embedded dispositions toward learning. What we have learned about the nature and power of the bond between significant adults and children through the work of John Bowlby (1988) is also critical to these interrelationships and is explored in the following section.

Attachment

From the discussion above we can see that children's early years are a critical time in which the foundations for healthy development are laid. Positive stimulation early in life affects subsequent health and well-being, and abundant research demonstrates that experiences from conception to age 6 have the most important influence on connecting and sculpting the neurons in children's brains.

Positive parent–child relationships are at the core of children's well-being and our attention is constantly drawn to the importance of consistent, nurturing and dependable relationships in shaping children's developmental outcomes. Advancing the earlier work of Bowlby (1988), there is much literature that explains the importance of young children's attachment relationships, first with their parents or primary carers and then with significant others (see, for example, Appleyard and Berlin, 2007; Jordan and Sketchley, 2009). Attachment theory emphasises the patterns and quality of infant–parent relationships and their influence on developing children's senses of identity and well-being.

There are many authors who criticise attachment theory because of its predominant focus on mothers, which they believe perpetuates 'mother blame' and 'mother guilt'. They believe that it is through the constructs of 'responsible mother' and 'fragile child' that an 'expert' view of child-rearing has been embedded and individual rather than systemic responsibility for societal problems emphasised (Vanobbergen, et al. 2006). Although these are criticisms that are indeed upheld in this book, from a service delivery perspective some aspects of the attachment view on human relationships enables a deeper understanding of child and parent behaviour in some settings. In particular it provides a useful conceptual tool for examining parent–child interaction in programmes which are designed for young children and parents to participate in together. With this in mind, the concepts of secure and 'letting go' behaviours from attachment theory and the development of repertoires of practice (Rogoff, et al. 2007) will be discussed in depth in Chapter 3 with a particular focus on 0–3-year-olds.

Joint understanding

Colwyn Trevarthen's work has illustrated the inherent social nature of children's learning and in particular the importance of the pairing or dyad of the mother and child (Trevarthen, 2011) in facilitating the development of this social disposition. Trevarthen's (1998) elaboration of the concept of intersubjectivity is often employed in relation to adult mediation of children's learning (Jordan, 2004; Rogoff, 1990; Wertsch, 2007).

Intersubjectivity is identified with a model of adult mediation and co-construction of meaning, which sees adults attuned to the children's intentions not only through language, but also through gesture, posture, tone and context (Göncü, 1998). Of the 18-month-old child Trevarthen notes a great deal of familiar household objects being treated as what they are, that is, signifying the child's at least partial grasp of the social functions of objects. He also notes;

> the toddler's play may seem egocentric, because the child characteristically turns his back to the mother most of the time and may shrug off any recommendation she may have to offer as to what should be done with the

toys and may say 'No!' to her. However, what the mother shows or says is picked up and does influence what the toddler attends to and plays with. (Trevarthen, 1998: 96)

These types of observations illustrate a tension in interpreting children's learning, do children learn through personal exploration or through social mediation? Trevarthen proceeds to outline how toddlers' ability to share experiences with others is influenced by the richness of previous shared experiences. He points to language limitations in children as old as 3 years leading to episodes of shared imitation in play. He highlights the ability of toddlers to imitate play and speech but stresses: 'Getting beyond this mimicry of speech sounds to using language to think and plan needs the backing of other people who are willing to join in games of give and take with words' (Trevarthen, 1998: 96).

The foundations for shared learning Reddy (2001) begin in an early perceptory disposition that focuses infants' attention on eyes and eye direction. This facilitates an early preoccupation with dyadic interactions that establish an awareness of gaze and attention by 6 months. However he suggests that it is not until 12 months of age that infants can use adult gaze for the precise location of a target, an observation also supported by Camaioni (2001). Reddy (2001) identifies the revolution children experience in understanding others' intentions around the age of 8 to 14 months not just because infants are more able to act on the world, but because they are also more able to engage with the way the world is presented to them by others (Reddy, 2001).

Joint attention is clearly a basic building block of social learning. It leads and accompanies a growing understanding of intentions which are based initially on movement. This understanding becomes increasingly sophisticated so that by 18 months infants react differently when approached by adults, often with more anxiety and thoughtfulness (Lock, 2001).

Bornstein and Tamis-Lemonda (2001) indentify many functions in the dyadic parent–child relationship. In particular they place significant focus on promotion of social understanding, development of attachment, acquisition and emotional regulation: 'From birth babies appear both ready and motivated (albeit in rudimentary form) to communicate and share meaning with others. By two months of age infants engage in complex, highly responsive interactions with their mothers termed "protoconversations"' (Bornstein and Tamis-Lemonda, 2001: 270).

They also suggest four types of caregiving:

- *nurturant* (supporting the immediate physical and emotional needs of the child);
- *social* (developing emotional, physical and intellectual skills to facilitate social interaction);

- *material* (controlling the physical environment of the child); and
- *didactic* caregiving (guiding learning) an observation also noted by Rogoff (1998: 705):

> 'Mothers from some communities regulate joint attention in the first year, often following infants direction of gaze, by touching or shaking an indicated object, or introducing it between themselves and the infant. They often provide verbal and non verbal interpretation for babies' actions, their own actions and events in the environment.'

Rogoff (1998) gives examples of infant games such as 'Peek-boo' and 'All Gone' that include missing actions, sounds or words as well as meal-time routines that develop the social communicative constructs required to scaffold children's learning. Rogoff indicates a number of studies that show children are actively influencing their interactions with adults through eye contact, smiling and cooperating, and sustaining or not sustaining interest: 'From a social cultural perspective the question is not when intersubjectivity is acquired, but rather how it transforms as children and their social partners change' (Rogoff, 1998: 707).

Rogoff sees these types of interactions as consistent with Vygotsky's (1986) model of the zone of proximal development which suggests that cognitive development is shaped by social exchanges from birth and that this becomes more sophisticated as speech develops.

Lock (2001) summarises the skills that children have usually mastered by the end of the first year of life. He identifies that children:

- Execute intentions alone and in harness with others
- Coordinate objects and people together in pursuit of these intentions
- Use gestures to partly specify these intentions
- Subordinate his or her own actions to the regulatory control of a limited number of another's words
- Voluntarily give, take and request objects in interaction with others, and who has 'fined down' some control of his or her own repertoire of sound production. (Lock, 2001: 391)

Lock goes on to note how during the second year of life these skills are applied to a realisation that words or names refer to things. However he draws attention to the fact that there is not a universal sequence of stages that children naturally mature through and supports the idea that language emerges from a system of underlying competencies. He also supports the view that meaning is constructed from the environment but urges us to remember that children's environments are not perceived from the same perspective as adults'. Similarly Karpov (2005) summarises research illustrating how mothers' participation in object-focused play lengthens and socialises the function of objects leading to the increasing sophistication of imaginative play in the third year of life.

Well-being and positive learning dispositions

Indisputably, children's development is supported by positive, nurturing relationships with their parents or primary caregivers. Significantly, though, many authors' work differentiates between nurturing behaviours and the skills required to carry out parenting tasks. They emphasise that children need nurturing for optimal development (Berry and Letendre, 2004; Munford and Sanders, 2006). It is also clear that the ability to nurture children is reliant on the health and well-being of their parents (Barnes et al., 2006; Shonkoff and Phillips, 2000). Further, parents' own relational experiences impact on the ways in which they interact with their children and need to be duly considered (Berry and Letendre, 2004; Munford and Sanders, 2006). Taylor (2002) refers to nurturing as tending and illustrates the interconnections between parent support, tending and children's development as follows:

> We can think of human tending as like an onion in its structure. At the innermost layer is the mother and other constant caregivers, often the father. Immediately surrounding them are family and close friends who provide social support. Enveloping them is the neighbourhood and larger community that provides the resources on which good tending depends. Each layer protects those that lie closer to the core, first by providing a supportive environment that makes good tending possible and also by providing additional tending resources when they are needed. (Taylor, 2002: 72)

This quote again alerts us to the ecological influences on child and parent relationships. Stimulating, rich play environments and playful relationships can support strong relationships, secure self-image and support children's growth and development (Bodrova and Leong, 2007; Centre for Community Child Health, 2008; Pramling-Samuelsson and Fleer, 2009; Zigler and Bishop-Josef, 2009) and are recognised as the right of every child under the United Nations Convention on the Rights of the Child (Office of the United Nations High Commissioner for Human Rights, 1989).

More specifically, Smilansky and Shefatya (1990) in a review of numerous studies on play found that it contributes to verbalisation, vocabulary, language comprehension, imagination, concentration, impulse control, curiosity, problem-solving strategies, cooperation, empathy and group participation. Other authors have also pointed to the substantial benefits across all areas of development that play has for children's transition to formal schooling, particularly when combined with high-quality relationships (Centre for Community Child Health, 2008; Dockett and Perry, 2003; Woodrow and Jackson, 2008).

The importance of play to healthy relationships and learning in early childhood is emphasised in social constructivist accounts of child development (Ashton et al., 2008; Piaget and Inhelder, 1969; Vygotsky, 1978). This approach is characterised by the belief that children learn best in holistic environments in which they actively construct or co-construct meaning in real-life situations.

Children's play from a social constructivist perspective is examined in cross-cultural studies conducted by Rogoff et al. (2003, 2007) in which they articulate the processes by which children learn from participation and play in everyday activities with or alongside adults. These authors emphasise the value of co-participation between adults and young children in activities that are relevant to their particular cultures. Importantly, Pramling-Samuelsson and Fleer (2009) also alert scholars to the fact that play cannot be defined in one particular way and that most behaviours and activities of young children have been described as play by theorists at some stage.

The concept of dispositions (Brooker, in Waller et al., 2011) is tremendously helpful to those working with young children. Brooker traces the development of dispositions in the early childhood education literature to Katz. Dispositions are associated with habits, traits, attitudes, predispositions and learning styles which children bring to their engagement with activities. Clearly some children are more likely to respond with different levels of enthusiasm in response to a call to play ball or read a book.

All of the factors considered so far in this chapter point to the possibility of certain types of support enhancing children's capacity to develop habits of mind and body that will bring them increasing returns. The evidence in support of playful nurturing relationships leading to beneficial outcomes for children and the roles of parents and practitioners in nurturing positive dispositions is discussed in Chapter 3.

In the remainder of this chapter we exemplify some of the ideas that we have introduced through an example of a parent and child pair, or dyad, engaged in joint activity in a dual-focused group in a children's centre in England.

A case study example of a parent–child dyad

In this example Jamie-Lee (2 years 3 months) and her mother illustrate how young children can focus and concentrate for long periods where they are supported in pursuing their own interests. Lynn was a full-time mother approaching her mid-twenties, with two older children.

Jamie-Lee, 2 years 3 months

JL moves to a tray that contains plastic crockery, picks out a roll of blue tape and a pair of scissors that she had placed there earlier and pulls out a 30 cm length of tape.

'Shall we cut some?' asks her mum, Lynn, who takes the tape reel and holds it out with a length of tape extended for JL to cut with the scissors.

'There's a good girl,' her mum offers as JL snips at the tape with a hand on each handle of the scissors. 'Waaay!' says mum as a piece of tape separates from the reel 'there's a good girl.'

'Sticked' says JL as the tape curls up and sticks together. JL tries to cut another piece with her mum still holding the tape.

'That's it, if you do a little cut.' Lynn holds up a pair of scissors for JL to see. 'Open shut. Open shut.'

'Let me see you do it a little cut and then pull the tape.' JL succeeds in cutting another long piece of tape. 'One last piece, we don't want to waste too much.'

JL moves all the way around the area dividers to pick up some crinkly scissors from the collage area where the tape and scissors are out on tables. She brings the scissors to her mum and offers them to her because the teeth are locked together. 'Are they stuck?' says mum as she tries to open them. While some of the adults open up the scissors JL picks up a reel of transparent tape and pulls out a length of tape which breaks off, then JL crinkles it up. She tries to pull another length of tape but the tape is stuck down and she smiles to her mother and offers the reel to her saying 'here'. She goes back to the shelves and chooses a reel of masking tape and pulls off another long strip then puts the reel down on the shelves next to mum. JL finds another roll of tape but it is also stuck down and so she chooses a reel of red tape. 'Red tape have you got red tape, red.' JL chooses some red handled scissors. 'They are red scissors to go with your red tape. Put your fingers in there,' and Lynn guides JL's fingers into the scissors so that she could use one hand: 'Open and shut, open and shut.'

Lynn holds the tape for JL to cut and JL goes back to holding the scissors with two hands but this time with the point facing down and cuts two or three pieces of tape. 'Mum, mum,' she says passing the scissors to her mother.

Jamie-Lee is absorbed in cutting lengths of different coloured sticky tape to make bracelets, an activity she had engaged in before with her mother at the group. Lynn was keenly aware of this interest and Jamie-Lee's strong desire to persist and master it. She gives her plenty of space and time allowing her to take responsibility for the activity but she is there to minimise frustration in managing the scissors and the sticky tape when needed. Carr (2001) argues that positive dispositions to taking responsibility and persisting are among the key learning dispositions that practitioners should be seeking to nurture in pre-school settings.

In the example which follows, Lynn adopts a more leading role but this is still negotiated with Jamie-Lee as they seek to agree the joint focus of their attention.

Jamie-Lee, 2 years 3 months

Jamie-Lee is kneeling on the floor next to a tray of sand. She is filling a white bucket with sand using a spade. Her mum sits down next to her. 'Cake' says Jamie-Lee.

'That's a good idea,' says her mum, 'put the sand in there first.' They both scoop sand into the bucket and then tip out the sand. 'Oh dear,' says mum laughing as it falls flat. 'Shall we try mixing some water in and see what that does?' Mum takes the bucket and asks if it is OK to put a little water in the sand which she does, creating a small strip of wet sand. 'Let's try that sand and see what happens.' They both put sand into the white bucket and then mum turns the bucket over and lifts off the bucket revealing a well-formed shape on the sand. 'Yeaay, it worked!' says mum. JL swings her hand and chops a corner off the top of the castle and then with another chop knocks the 'cake' down.

'Would you like a book now?' asks Lynn and she moves around the other side of the dividing shelves. JL continues half filling the bucket with sand. 'Jamie-Lee would you like a book now?' JL moves to the opposite side of the sand tray so she can see her mother more easily but continues to fill the bucket. Her mother comes back next to her and says 'Remember which one made a sandcastle, remember the wet one.' Mum starts to fill a transparent bucket with sand while JL continues to fill the white bucket. JL stands up with the bucket of sand and moves towards her mother. 'Do you need some taps on the bottom? Shall we tip it? One … two … three.' Again the sand tips out of the bucket but they both note that the sand can now be seen halfway up the inside of the bucket. Lynn encourages JL to touch the wet sand. 'It is cold and wet, look at that one it runs through your fingers, hold your hand out and it falls, try this one [dry sand] it doesn't make a ball. Can you do it with the wet sand?' JL does this and holds the ball of sand in her palm. 'Ball' she says.

'Have you made a ball?' asks her mum.

This episode also suggests that Jamie-Lee's positive dispositions are being nurtured, she is offered the chance to lead the activity and control the pace and direction. She is offered and accepts ideas, and maintains a shared communicative space with her mother responding non-verbally throughout and verbally at the end. Curiosity and enjoyment is promoted throughout the episode, along with use of words to classify and reflect on particular aspects of the experience.

When asked about her role in supporting Jamie-Lee, Lynn said:

Erm I sort of try to give her ideas but she has definitely got her own little head on her shoulders and she knows what she wants to do and sometimes no matter what I say to her she has got her own little thing going on. She doesn't always take on board what I am saying but I am there for her if she needs me more than anything. I think I have realised I have got to take a bit of a back seat in whatever she does and just let her get on with it. It's nice, it gives me a bit of a break and a chance for a bit of a chit chat without having to worry about being there for her all the time.' (Lynn, mother)

Lynn's comments suggest that she sees Jamie-Lee's eagerness for some independence in pursuing her interests as a positive disposition which she is happy to nurture along with creativity and enquiry:

It's a different approach to play [at this stay and play group] a lot of the time they give you the usual dolls, slides and so on in the groups I have been to in the past. There is a lot more creative play here, that gives the children a chance to make their own play activities instead of having something set for them. It's good for their development I think. Not many places offer tape for them to do cutting and that definitely seems to be her favourite thing at the moment. (Lynn, mother)

 Reflective activities: supporting the development of learning dyads

This chapter has demonstrated how young children actively construct their view of the world through their experiences. We have shown that young children in particular experience the world holistically combing sensory, emotional and cognitive dimensions in ways which are often recalled by later encounters with the same or similar materials. It has been suggested that parents or other adults are often the main mediators and facilitators of children's engagement and participation in activities, and that this helps children shape their attitudes towards activities and learning.

1. Reflect on the case study of Jamie-Lee and Lynn. What are the potential psychological and emotional benefits of Lynn's approach for Jamie-Lee?
2. Think of a child that you work with and identify how his/her positive dispositions are nurtured by the activities available in your setting.

Try developing a diagram which identifies the most influential ecological influences on a group you are involved in.

References

Appleyard, K. and Berlin, L. (2007) 'Supporting healthy relationships between young children and their parents: lessons from attachment theory and research', accessed 17 October 2009 at http://sanford.duke.edu/centers/child/eca/Attachment/index.htm.

Ashton, J., Woodrow, C., Johnston, C., Wangmann, J., Singh, L. and James, T. (2008) 'Partnerships in learning: linking early childhood services, families and schools for optimal development', *Australian Journal of Early Childhood*, 33(2): 10–16.

Athey, C. (2007) *Extending Thought in Young Children*. London: Sage.

Barnes, J., Leach, P., Sylva, K., Malmberg, L. and team TF (2006) 'Infant childcare: mother's aspirations, actual experiences and the predictors of their satisfaction and confidence in communication with caregivers', *Early Child Development and Care*, 127(5): 533–73.

Berry, M. and Letendre, J. (2004) 'Lambs and lions: the role of psychoeducational groups in enhancing relationship skills and social networks', *Groupwork*, 14(1): 30–45.

Bodrova, E. and Leong, D. (2007) *Tools of the Mind. The Vygotskian Approach to Early Childhood Education*. Upper Saddle River, NJ: Pearson Education.

Bornstein, M.H. and Tamis-Lemonda, C.S. (2001) 'Mother-infant interaction', in G.J. Bremner and A. Fogel (eds), *Blackwell Handbook of Infant Development*. Malden, MA: Blackwell. pp. 269–295.

Bowlby, J. (1988) *A Secure Base: Clinical Applications of Attachment Theory*. London: Routledge.

Bronfenbrenner, H. (1979) *The Ecology of Human Development*. Cambridge, MA: Harvard University Press.

Brooker, L. (2011) 'Learning dispositions for life', in T. Waller, J. Whitmarsh and K. Clarke (eds), *Making Sense of Theory and Practice in Early Childhood: The Power of Ideas*. Maidenhead: Open University Press.

Camaioni, L. (2001) 'Early language', in G.J. Bremner and A. Fogel (eds), *Blackwell Handbook of Infant Development*. Malden, MA: Blackwell.

Carr, M. (2001) *Assessment in Early Childhood Settings*. London: Paul Chapman Publishing.

Centre for Community Child Health. (2008) 'Rethinking the transition to school: Linking schools and early years services', Policy brief no. 11, accessed on 2 November 2008 at www.rch.org.au/ccch/policybriefs.cfm.

Darwin, C. (1928) *The Origin of Species*. London: Dent.

Dawkins, R. (2004) *The Ancestor's Tale*. London: Weidenfeld and Nicolson.

Dockett, S. and Perry, B. (2003) 'The transition to school: what's important?', *Educational Leadership*, 60(7): 30–33.

Göncü, A. (1998) 'Development of intersubjectivity in social pretend play', in M. Woodhead, D. Faulkner and L. Karen (eds), *Cultural Worlds of Early Childhood*. London: Routledge.

Goswami, U. (2008) *Cognitive Development: The Learning Brain*. Hove: Psychology Press.

Jordan, B. (2004) 'Scaffolding learning and co-constructing understandings', in A. Anning, J. Cullen and M. Fleer (eds), *Early Childhood Studies*. London: Paul Chapman Publishing.

Jordan, B. and Sketchley, R. (2009) 'A stitch in time saves nine: preventing and responding to the abuse and neglect of infants', *Child Abuse Prevention Issues*, 30, accessed 2 August 2009 at www.aifs.gov.au/nch/pubs/issues/issues30/issues30.html.

Karpov, Y.V. (2005) *The Neo-Vygotskian Approach to Child Development*. New York: Cambridge University Press.

Leont'ev, A.N. (1978) *Activity, Consciousness, and Personality*. Englewood Cliffs, NJ: Prentice-Hall.

Lock, A. (2001) 'Preverbal communication', in G.J. Bremner and A. Fogel (eds), *Blackwell Handbook of Infant Development*. Malden, MA: Blackwell.

Mareschal, D., Johnson, M. and Grayson, A. (2004) *Brain and Cognitive Development*. Milton Keynes: Open University Press.

Maybin, J. and Woodhead, M. (2003) *Childhoods in Context*. Milton Keynes: Open University Press.

Munford, R. and Sanders, J. (2006) *Strengths-based Social Work with Families*. Melbourne: Thomson.

Office of the United Nations High Commissioner for Human Rights (1989) 'Convention on the rights of the child', General assembly resolution 44/25, accessed 31 October 2009 at www.unhchr.ch/html/menu3/b/k2crc.htm.

Piaget, J. (1950) *The Psychology of Intelligence*. London: Routledge Kegan Paul.

Piaget, J. and Inhelder, B. (1969) *The Psychology of the Child*. London: Routledge and Kegan Paul.

Pinker, S. (2002) *The Blank Slate: The Modern Denial of Human Nature*. London: Allen Lane.

Pramling-Samuelsson, I. and Fleer, M. (2009) *Play and Learning in Early Childhood Settings*. Fankston: Springer.

Reddy, V. (2001) 'Mind knowledge in the first year: understanding attention and intention', in G.J. Bremner and A. Fogel (eds), *Blackwell Handbook of Infant Development*. Malden, MA: Blackwell.

Rogoff, B. (1990) *Apprenticeship Thinking in the Social Context*. New York: Open University Press.

Rogoff, B. (1998) 'Cognition as a collaborative process', in D. Kuhn and R.S. Siegler (eds), *Handbook of Child Psychology*. New York: Wiley and Sons.

Rogoff, B., Moore, L., Najafi, B., Dexter, A., Correa-Chavez, M. and Solis, J. (2007) 'Children's development of cultural repertoires through participation in everyday routines and practices', in J.E. Grusec and P.D. Hastings (eds), *Handbook of Socialisation: Theory and Research*. New York: The Guilford Press. pp. 490–515.

Rogoff, B., Paradise, R., Mejia Arauz, R., Correa-Chavez, M. and Angelillo, C. (2003) 'Firsthand learning through intent participation', *Annual Review of Psychology*, 54: 175–203.

Sharot, T. (2012) *Science Club: Reproduction*, BBC 2 Television, viewed 23 December 2012.

Shonkoff, J. and Phillips, D. (2000) *From Neurons to Neighborhoods.* Washington, DC: National Academy Press.

Smilansky, S. and Shefatya, L. (1990) *Facilitating Play: A Medium for Promoting Cognitive, Socio-emotional, and Academic Development in Young Children.* Gaithersburg, MD: Psychological and Educational Publications.

Taylor, S. (2002) *The Tending Instinct.* New York: Times Books Henry Holt and Company.

Trevarthen, C. (1998) 'The child's need to learn a culture', in M. Woodhead, D. Faulkner and L. Karen (eds), *Cultural Worlds of Early Childhood.* London: Routledge.

Trevarthen, C. (2011) 'What young children give to their learning, making education work to sustain a community and its culture', *European Early Childhood Education Research Journal,* 19(2).

Vanobbergen, B., Vandenbroeck, M., Roose, R. and Bouverne-De Bie, M. (2006) '"We are one big, happy family": Beyond negotiation and compulsory happiness', *Educational Theory,* 56(4): 423–37.

Vygotsky, L.S. (1978) *Mind in Society.* Cambridge, MA: Harvard University Press.

Vygotsky, L.S. (1986) *Thought and Language.* Cambridge, MA: MIT Press.

Wertsch, J.V. (2007) '*Vygotsky on Human Nature and Human Development',* keynote address at the 17th European Early Childhood Education Research Association Annual Conference, Prague, 29 August to 1 September.

Woodrow, C. and Jackson, D. (2008) 'Connections for learning: the role of supported playgroups in supporting transitions to school', paper presented at the 18th European Early Childhood Education Research Association Annual Conference, Stavanger, Norway.

Zigler, E. and Bishop-Josef. (2009) 'Play under siege', *Zero to Three,* 30(1): 5–11.

CHAPTER 2

Researching with families

Chapter overview

In this chapter we consider some ways in which engaging with parents in reflective research may form the basis of meaningful and mutually beneficial activities. Research can lead to a deeper level of cooperation and knowledge exchange that benefits parents and practitioners, as well as children. The chapter begins by summarising key examples of working in partnership with parents to develop shared knowledge. The chapter sets out a short justification for adopting a commitment to research informed practice and recommends a sociocultural research approach and feminist ethical principles to support this. Examples of observations and interviews involving parents are used to illustrate the type of methods that are likely to be helpful in developing reflective practice with parents.

Introduction

We begin by highlighting a number of projects that have adopted a co-reflective approach to practice with families and which continue to inspire and lead this field. These projects demonstrate the potential of shared processes in which both parties learn to value the knowledge that each has to contribute. These processes demonstrate the potential of reflective research to identify new learning among adult stakeholders as well as children.

Practice at Pen Green in the UK has been at the forefront of Children's Centre leadership and research partnerships with parents in particular (Whalley and the Pen Green Team, 2007). Tait (2007) outlined Pen Green's core 'Growing Together' offer that invites parents and children under three to participate jointly:

> To give parents a chance to play with their child;
> To help parents understand more about their relationship with their child;
> To dialogue with parents about their children's development;
> To encourage reflective parenting (through reflecting on video material);
> To facilitate parent-to-parent support;
> To validate the feeling women are experiencing, when they suffer from postnatal depression;
> To reinforce helpful attachment experiences. (Tait, 2007: 142)

The team at Pen Green have documented practice that illustrates how involving parents as co-educators and researchers in the investigation of their children's learning has positive impacts on the interactions between parents and children and between parents and practitioners. They emphasise a cognitive as well as caring dimension to the parents' role (Whalley and the Pen Green Team, 2007).

Tait (2007) also highlights how video and discussion has been harnessed to raise awareness of the emotional and responsive nature of parent–child relationships. Parents are involved as partners in reflecting on the interpretation and anticipation of children's activities and interests, through reflection on observed and recorded activities. This is an interpretative approach informed by research and selected through ongoing study and experiences.

In Australia, Connect Child and Family Services implements reflective research approaches across its broad range of early childhood and family service provision (Jackson, 2010). Parent-led conversation is one ethnographic method routinely used across the organisation to reflect with parents on the service they or their children are attending. Purposeful conversation often leads to new knowledge which, in turn, leads to child and family-centred programme changes or the co-creation of new service delivery.

One recent example highlights the use of this methodology in the development of a new home-visiting programme for parents of very young children. During a parent-led conversation between a supported playgroup facilitator and a parent in a regular playgroup session, the parent shared her experience of being sleep deprived from parenting a young child. She also shared her knowledge about what would be supportive for parents such as herself in this situation. As a result this parent worked alongside the playgroup facilitator to scope the idea of a new parent support programme which has now been established and which employs the parent as a part time coordinator.

A third inspiration comes from the work of Tobin (2005) who used video to facilitate focus group reflection on practice and context. In the Crossing Borders project (Kurban and Tobin, 2009) he employed video as a basis for focus group discussions across five countries, and the recordings were analysed to enable the exploration of multivocal, inter-cultural dialogue.

In this case focus groups of parents in the different countries viewed not only the video portraying their own country but also each of the others. Usually having only their own experiences to draw on, all participants found that sharing, comparing and reflecting on all their videos broadened their horizons, experience and insights.

If practitioners are planning to develop research activities with parents they will need to consider what type of research style and rules they will abide by. There are too many possibilities to go into detail here, however, we will highlight a few key starting points which are suited to the type of activities occurring in dual-focused groups.

A commitment to developing practice through research

When researchers are committed to research that informs a deeper understanding of children's circumstances, and can convey this honestly and transparently to parents, then improved relationships and insights for revised practice will follow. Pedagogy, in England, has traditionally been defined as the art and science of teaching. However, in Europe, and increasingly in early childhood education in Australia, pedagogy is used to refer to a more holistic and integrated view of raising children; a view that involves practitioners reflecting systematically on their own practice as well as research.

Such a definition is increasingly supported by the arguments and evidence presented in Chapter 1 which indicates that the emotional, cognitive, social and physical domains are strongly bound to each other in young children's activities. There is therefore a philosophical resonance to the idea that pedagogy is the construction of praxeological knowledge in situated action (Formosinho and Formosinho, 2012). Knowledge of child development and sociological perspectives need to be critically evaluated in the here and now of the activities practitioners engage with.

The Formoshinos identify transmissible pedagogies with practices that seek to replicate and conserve cultural practices over time through consistent and prescribed methods; for example, when structuring experiences designed to ensure that children learn to read. This is contrasted with participatory pedagogies which through greater emphasis on the exchange of information between individuals lead to the development of more creative approaches. In this book we agree that the practice of raising children occurs in community contexts. Therefore research which promotes increased awareness and understanding across the community, conforms with and broadens the exemplification of a participatory pedagogy offered by the Formosinhos.

🔑 Key idea: a sociocultural approach

Rogoff (2003) offers invaluable guidance to those considering how best to study interactions with young children in real-world contexts. She consistently highlights how culture impacts upon the way adults guide children's participation in activity, and argues that this process may shape general as well as specific learning attitudes. Rogoff (2003) indicates that there is a degree of negotiated reciprocity in social exchanges that enhances or restricts shared learning and these processes are moderated by culture and context.

Further Rogoff (2003) acknowledges the importance of cultural practices embedded in objects, language, gestures, and activities often referred to as cultural tools. She also identifies the difficulties of holding up a focusing lens that foregrounds each element of an activity at once. It is usually necessary to foreground some aspects of the phenomena and background others simply because no one can study everything at once. However, the distinctions between what is foreground and what is in the background lie in our analysis and are not assumed to be separate entities in reality (Rogoff, 2003: 58).

To aid the study of interactions Rogoff (2003) identifies three potential lenses that might be used: an individual focus, an interpersonal focus and a cultural institutional focus. In particular, this book presents examples of what Rogoff identifies as the interpersonal focus of analysis for investigating the way that adults support and reinforce children's engagement within particular social contexts. In our case these are activities and interactions that occur during dual-focused group sessions.

There are relatively few studies applying activity approaches in pedagogic contexts and even fewer focused on dual-focused provision such as parent and toddler groups. Past research has often focused on children aged 3 to 6 years located in educational contexts, observation suites and laboratories. With this in mind key publications by Hedegaard and Fleer (2008) and Pramling-Samuelsson and Fleer (2009) that discuss Rogoff's work are particularly helpful in refining the use of the concept of 'activity' in relation to the early education of toddlers.

In relation to dual-focused groups, theories examining sociocultural activity are particularly relevant because parents and practitioners have the ability to influence each other's views about how children's interests and explorations of activities can be supported. The study of interactions in these groups offers the potential for insight into how young children are encouraged to think about early education activities. It also offers the chance to see the extent to which children are encouraged to rely on their own responses to events, the extent to which they are encouraged to share their thinking with those around them, or the extent to which others thinking is imposed upon them.

Because sociocultural researchers are committed to study activity in practice, they frequently look to ethnographic researchers for guidance. Fetterman (1989) describes ethnography as the art and science of describing a group or culture. Ethnography affords the researcher the opportunity to record the attitudes and dispositions of those involved in a specific context. It takes time to try to see things from participants' perspectives and to check their interpretations of what takes place in that context focusing on daily routines of people to identify patterns of behaviour (Fetterman, 1989). The purpose here is to describe the exchanges between several differently culturally enabled groups; children, parents and early years practitioners. Fetterman (1989: 1) continues: 'the ethnographer enters the field with an open mind, not an empty head, before asking questions in the field, the ethnographer begins with a problem, a theory or model, a research design, specific data collection techniques specific data collection techniques, tools for analysis and a specific writing style'.

Recommended further reading

Hedegaard, M. and Fleer, M. (2008) *Studying Children: A Cultural-Historical Approach.* Maidenhead: Open University Press.

Those seeking to explore children's learning with parents need to be prepared with ideas about what they might find before they begin their observations and interviews. Denscombe (2007) characterises ethnography as attempting to examine and enter the culture of a group and endeavouring to present their perspectives on the activities they engage in (Denscombe, 2007). He also suggests that ethnographic accounts are recognised as an account constructed by the researcher and reflect something of the researcher and not a simple objective picture of the culture of the group studied. With this in mind, an ethnographic approach is helpful because it suggests an openness of mind towards the perspectives of the various stakeholders in the groups being studied. For practitioners studying their own practice, ethnography implies and reflects the researcher being immersed in the context of study.

Ethics

A trusting working partnership requires an appropriate ethical approach and we have found the position of the feminist communitarian researcher (Lincoln, in Fontana and Frey, 2003: 96) to be very helpful:

> there is a growing realisation that interviewers are not the mythical, neutral tools envisioned by survey research. Interviewers are increasingly seen as active participants in interactions with respondents, and interviews are seen as negotiated accomplishments of both interviewers and respondents that are shaped by the contexts in which they take place.
>
> This framework presumes a researcher who builds collaborative, reciprocal, trusting and friendly relations with those studied ... It is also understood that those studied have claims of ownership over any materials that are produced in the research process including field notes.

The Australian association for active educational researchers ethical guidelines advance four basic principles that are also helpful and clear:

1. The consequences of a piece of research, including the effects on the participants and the social consequences of its publication and application must enhance the general welfare.
2. Researchers should be aware of the variety of human goods and the variety of views on the good life, and the complex relation of education with these. They should recognise that educational research is an ethical matter, and that its purpose should be the development of human good.
3. No risk of significant harm to an individual is permissible unless either that harm is remedied or the person is of age and has given informed consent to the risk. Public benefit, however great, is insufficient justification.
4. Respect for the dignity and worth of persons and the welfare of students, research participants, and the public generally shall take precedence over self-interest of researchers, or the interests of employers, clients, colleagues or groups. (AARE, 2013)

Parents' viewpoints should be portrayed in a way that presents the spirit of their views clearly. To achieve this, transcripts of observations and conversations can be shared and verified to demonstrate respect and rigour.

While some researchers may suggest that the process of seeking informed consent from participants can undermine trusting relationships (Denzin and Lincoln, 2003). Many feel uncomfortable with the idea of dispensing with informed consent forms because this provides a useful process check. The consent process makes the researcher explain the way information will be collected and used and try to explain these to the group. The consent forms used are not binding upon the parent and the possibility of withdrawal and control should be made clear. With regard to children, while informed consent may be sought through the parents this must be with the assurance that if distress or discomfort is caused by the observation process that it will be suspended and reviewed.

Many early childhood authors argue that children's rights should be more fully acknowledged than has been the case in previous educational research and in the British Educational Research Association (BERA) guidelines (Harcourt and Conroy, 2005, Whalley et al., 2007). We would agree with the principle of seeking informed consent with children described by Harcourt and Conroy (2005) but with very young children this is not easy. However, even with young children assent can be sought to note taking which might include allowing them to inspect and write in notebooks. Children can also be asked through gesture if their picture can be taken; they can also be included in the sharing of documented observations.

Data collection techniques

Ideas for observation

The example which follows is intended to illustrate how observations of everyday events can become sharper and more informative if we slow them down and reflect on them through an appropriate set of ideas. The important thing is to have a systematic and informed process because, in doing so, themes and patterns begin to emerge. The intention of the process is to focus on different modes of interaction.

The following is an extract from a longer narrative observation that was carried out over a whole parent and toddler group session. It employs the learning story format developed in New Zealand by Carr (2001) which is firmly located in the sociocultural paradigm. The format emphasises that 'the focus is on the individual in action mediated by social partners, social practices and tools' (Carr, 2001: 8).

This framework was used for helping to structure an initial observation of the child but it was adapted to include reviewing how the adults' actions relate to the child's activity. Initial pocketbook notes were then written into an initial learning story within 24 hours of the initial observation. Carr's model of a learning story is adapted here to become a single multiple narrative describing three perspectives in parallel and overlapping stories considering each of the aspects in Figure 2.1.

Taking an interest	Being involved	Persistence with difficulty or uncertainty	Expressing an idea or a feeling	Taking responsibility
Child Parents Practitioners	Child Parents Practitioners	Child Parents Practitioners	Child Parents Practitioners	Child Parents Practitioners

Figure 2.1 Carr's key learning dispositions used to structure shared learning stories (after Carr, 2001)

Hedegaard and Fleer (2008: 49) commend the learning story format as an accessible and common sense tool 'acting as a record of the researcher's meaningful understanding as created through this interaction that becomes the data'. The story was then shared and verified and extended with the parent and practitioners.

Example observation: Ejaz (15 months)

As soon as they arrive his mum asks if the water activity is still going on and mum helps Ejaz to find an apron and to put it on. He stands by a pan that an older child has placed a waterwheel inside and his mum holds his hand and guides him in pouring water from a small blue cup over the waterwheel. Ejaz smiles broadly as the water flows over the wheel making it spin around. Mum continues to support this for several minutes and then Ejaz continues to spin the wheel using his hand. Ejaz struggles to reach inside the pan to the shapes and containers inside, he takes the shapes and passes them to his mum. She asks for the star and draws his attention to the star by holding it out to show him saying 'good boy'. Ejaz seems to share the connection between this word and the yellow star shaped pastry cutter. 'Star chaieya' [can I have the star please] Ejaz picks out the star again from a red bowl next to the pan. 'Cross chaieya ... 'Hexagon chaieya' says mum as he hands her other objects and she shows and names them back to him.

'Ejaz star, chaieya star.'

'Star' says Ejaz handing his mother the star.

'Good boy', she says enthusiastically and smiling.

There are several shapes in a red bowl that mum offers to Ejaz and she asks him to picks objects from the bowl which she guides 'square dad oh' [pass the square], 'hexagon dad oh, cup dah doh, Ysme[this thing] da doh' as Ejaz passes the objects from the bowl and drops them into the pan. Again, when she says 'star dado', Ejaz selects the appropriate shape and she smiles and says 'good boy'. 'Missed' she says as the objects that Ejaz is dropping back into the pan misses and lands on the floor, he picks up the cup and gives it a tentative lick.

'Ne ne [no no]' says mum. Ejaz cannot now reach the objects in the bottom of the pan and Martin helps her to move the pan to a chair so Ejaz can see inside. Another child has started playing on a piano and Ejaz pauses to look for where the sound is coming from. Mum holds a blue cup and Ejaz takes objects from the pan and places into the blue cup.

Taking an interest
Ejaz is comfortable to participate; investigating activities with his mother, sometimes joining her ideas and sometimes his own. He also likes to see what others are doing.

Being involved
Ejaz is happy to become involved in the activities offered by mum, he is comfortable to separate from mum at snack time and eager to be part of the story-time group with mum.

Persisting
Ejaz sustains and develops play in partnership with his mother with both the water and skittle activities.

Expressing ideas
Ejaz responds confidently to the questions posed by his mum, offering objects and gestures. He is starting to use a few words and sounds to make points more clearly.

Taking responsibility
Ejaz works with his mother to take some activities in the direction he wishes but also pleased to follow his mum's suggestions.

Ultimately the aim of all observation techniques is making the learning in everyday activities more visible to all those participating. To achieve this, a level of detail about factors key to the topic being investigated is critical. This observation identifies the tools being used, whether objects or ideas and shows how these tools are negotiated between the subjects participating in the activity. Those framing any investigation will need to reflect carefully to identify the key factors that need to be recorded in an observation in order to gain the insights they are seeking.

In the example given here the mother leads the child's activity but the child is a willing and enthusiastic participant. The activity offered by the mother appears to overlap with the child's interests. In the interview which follows shortly, she gives an insight into her view of her role in supporting his activity. In the research project reported here parents said it made them think more about how much their children were learning all the time: 'Especially after reading the observation last week. I didn't realise just how much she was learning when she was just playing. The things that she's doing by herself, the things I have been saying to her does all help with her learning. Things you wouldn't think about normally' (parent).

Videos offer the advantage of capturing many aspects of a situation in much greater detail and can be very powerful when shared with the participants in that context. While the benefits are clear, video will take time to set up and get used to. Video can cause participants to opt out, and it can be uncomfortable to view as well as time-consuming to edit. Video still requires careful attention to deciding what key factors need to be recorded to ensure that filming is focused at the right place, at the right time.

Photographs combined with written observations can make a useful alternative to video because this may be a less intrusive process particularly if it is already common practice in the group. Where photographs or videos are used, then permissions regarding taking and using them will need to be considered. Photographs do help to stimulate recall for all the parties involved in a particular moment in time and the context of the activity around it. Sharing permissions, data storage and contemplating the length of time something may be kept, all also require careful consideration.

Interviews

Learning stories whether in written, video, photographic, audio or aural form lend themselves to Kvale's Process typology for interviews (Wengraf, 2001), which involves introducing questions in the context of asking the interviewees to recall a particular occasion. The 'rich spontaneous descriptions' (Wengraf, 2001: 170) of activity might then be followed with probing, specifying, direct, indirect and interpretive questions. A potential difficulty with this strategy is that it may lead to an asymmetrical trust interview: 'In the asymmetrical trust interview, the interviewer is described as sage, as a source of counsel and wisdom, and the interviewee as petitioner, holding the weak side of a power balance' (Wengraf, 2001: 153).

If the intention of the research is to try to elicit parents' and practitioners' insights into children, it may be useful to keep professional analytical comments separate. If the intention is to strive for an interview where an even relationship (Wengraf, 2001) is sought, then emphasising the interviewees' knowledge as valuable and increasingly opening up the ideas of the researcher in the later parts of interviews encourages a more open exchange of ideas.

An example of an individual interview
This example is intended to illustrate the potential value of interviews that are rooted in observations. If interviews can build on relationships established through the ethnographic principles and the open approach described earlier in this chapter, the invitation to share experiences through open questions can lead to full and open responses to questions. Following informal discussions and support offered to her child's play in previous sessions, and having shared the learning story presented in the previous section, Shafiqa shared her perspectives on how the play sessions fitted in with play at home. The aim of these conversations was to explore the parent's and practitioner's perspectives on their roles in supporting the child's development as a learner, in order to explore the way that they described their approach to supporting learning.

Shafiqa (Ejaz's mother)

How do activities fit in with your child's wider interests? Are there things that Ejaz does here that he doesn't do at home?
The water play was one thing, obviously I do water play with things at home and the water went absolutely everywhere and obviously because of my condition, expecting any time, I can't do many things with him at home that are activity based, you know running about going out and stuff but I do try and do activities with him at home. Once you have a small child then you are confined to small space aren't you? There's the living room and our garden's not huge either so I also want him to see other children as well he doesn't get much chance at home.

Why come to the group?
I bring him here mainly because I want him to do activities that you can't do at home like the water play activities and many of the activities that they have during the summer. He's an only child at the moment. I take him to my relatives, I want him to see children more frequently and he doesn't have any brothers and sisters at home. I mean he enjoys it as well. I've seen children who are quite clingy to their mothers and I don't want him to be like that. I want him to be very independent to be able to sit down on his own amongst other children. It is amazing sometimes I'll do things and he'll copy me straight away and others times I'll encourage him and he won't want to do it because he doesn't want to do it. They like to take things at

(Continues)

(Continued)

their own pace don't they in doing things. Yeah I mean ideally it's better to do things in the playgroup that he can't do at home. I can do reading at home, I can do rhymes and stuff, I do like doing activities with him, I'll sit down and we'll make a frog for instance that is one to one; this is a big group isn't it he needs to be able to play both ways. I do a story with him at home. I realise he probably listens more attentively to me at home cause I'm speaking to him directly; when he's in a group he won't sit so attentively he'll just like look at the other children, he won't look at the book specifically, he looks at objects randomly. And he won't listen to the story.

How do you see your role at the group?
I think I am more in like a support role really, support. I need to guide him most of the time through activities; they take less notice of their mums and their carers and more notice of teachers if their teachers ask questions they'll probably look around. I do try and provide it [support] but I also do try and play with him as well with activities. I use the opportunity to like spend time with him as well.

The interviewers role is to create a situation where the topic for discussion and questions asked are meaningful to the interviewee. The right questions in the right context combined with an established relationship which has demonstrated interest and a willingness to listen, will most likely result in an extended thoughtful response to a short question.

Focus groups

Focus groups can also be a very effective way to gather qualitative data because it presents a more natural conversational environment in which participants influence and are influenced by others (Krueger and Casey, 2000). Focus groups provide a social context where participants generate multiple and diverse understandings of the subject through collaborative dialogue. The researcher plays the role of questioner, moderator, listener and observer in order to promote purposeful conversations that bring the researcher closer to the subject matter through direct and personal encounter (Krueger and Casey, 2000; McLachlan, 2005).

The goal of focus groups in research is to provide a comfortable, permissive environment that facilitates the gathering of rich data. For this to occur, however, it is necessary to pay attention to factors that promote self-disclosure among participants, thus allowing the researcher to better understand what participants think and feel. Krueger and Casey (2000) identify group size, participant similarities and group location as being critical in the promotion of self-disclosure in focus groups. To this end, they recommend groups to be formed with more than six but no more than 12 participants who share a common experience. They also recommend that groups are held in locations where participants will be comfortable and at ease. Krueger and Casey (2000) also identify risk factors that may inhibit self-disclosure among focus group participants. They suggest that participants in the group need to identify as closely as possible with the moderator or facilitator of the group to avoid the perception of a power differential which may limit participation.

The following excerpts from a research focus group illustrate the potential of shared reflection.

Case study

Researcher: The parents here seem quite focused compared to other groups there are not many 'off children' conversations?

Practitioner K: Come to our Wednesday afternoon sessions, because they are a bit that way at the minute aren't they? Because you never have two groups the same. We've got a clique at the moment and they are just sitting right on that sofa.

Practitioner A: Or they'll just sit on the couch and use the session to have a break while the child plays.

Practitioner C: But that might be their only break and there is only three or four families on a Wednesday afternoon. And unless their children get really unruly which is unlikely to happen because we wouldn't let it. It is alright for them to sit there. One is heavily pregnant and is due anytime.

Practitioner A: It is about moderation and having woman to woman time.

Researcher: There was a nice point in the discussion time about chalks and some reasons why it would be good to use the chalks outside because the children enjoyed them and they could do bigger things and mess didn't matter.

Practitioner C: Yes they all gave something that their children could enjoy doing in the end, they seemed to enjoy that large mark making activity with paint didn't they?

Practitioner B: Yeah Ejaz and Abigail.

Practitioner A: Abigail is really into paint anyway.

Practitioner B: And even though the aprons weren't out, their parents still let them explore. I said 'oh I've forgotten the aprons', and they just said 'oh it's too late now'. And when I took them out they did put them on but it didn't seem to make a difference to the parents. Which I thought was quite nice that the experience was more important than the clothes.

As in the individual interview example, the interviewer here listens carefully to the interviewees, and asks short, open, relevant questions in response to what has been said. The interview becomes a more genuine dialogue as compared to a fully structured interview and illustrates the tensions that practitioners can experience in facilitating the dual focus of the group.

 Reflective activities: parents and practitioners as co-researchers

This chapter has considered the value of adopting a praxeological partnership approach to working with parents. We have suggested a number of key issues which need to be reflected on in order to help structure research projects.

1. Identify a child that attends your setting who you would like to know better. What insights might you gain from working with a parent as a co-researcher?
2. Why would parents wish to participate in research with you? What insights might you have to offer to them? How would you invite them to join in a project and what things should you avoid if you want to keep them involved?
3. Reflect on the case study observation of Ejaz and the interview with Shafiqa. What issues or topics might you choose to investigate further?

References

Carr, M. (2001) *Assessment in Early Childhood Settings*. London: Paul Chapman Publishing.

Denscombe, M. (2007) *The Good Research Guide for Small Scale Social Research Projects*. Maidenhead: Open University Press.

Denzin, N.K. and Lincoln, Y.S. (2003) *Collecting and Interpreting Qualitative Materials*. Thousand Oaks, CA: Sage.

Fetterman, D.M. (1989) *Ethnography: Step by Step*. London: Sage.

Fontana, A. and Frey, J. (2003) 'The interview from structured questions to negotiated text', in N.K. Denzin and Y.S. Lincoln (eds), *Collecting and Interpreting Qualitative Materials*. Thousand Oaks, CA: Sage.

Formosinho, J. and Formosinho, J.O. (2012) 'Towards a social science of the social: the contribution of praxeological research', *European Early Childhood Education Research Journal*, 20(4): 591–606.

Harcourt, D. and Conroy, H. (2005) 'Informed assent: ethics and processes when researching with young children', *Early Child Development and Care*, 175(6): 567–77.

Hedegaard, M. and Fleer, M. (2008) *Studying Children: A Cultural-Historical Approach*. Maidenhead: Open University Press.

Jackson, D. (2010) 'A place to "be": supported playgroups a model of relational, social support for parents and children', University of Western Sydney, Sydney.

Krueger, R.A. and Casey, M.A. (2000) *Focus Groups: A Practical Guide for Applied Research*. London: Sage.

Kurban, F. and Tobin, J. (2009) '"They don't like us": reflections of Turkish children in a German preschool', *Contemporary Issues in Early Childhood*, 10(1): 24–34.

McLachlan, C. (2005) 'Focus group methodology and its usefulness in early childhood research', *New Zealand Research in Early Childhood Education*, 8: 113–21.

Pramling-Samuelsson, I. and Fleer, M. (2009) *Play and Learning in Early Childhood Settings*. Fankston: Springer.

Rogoff, B. (2003) *The Cultural Nature of Human Development*. Oxford: Oxford University Press.

Tait, C. (2007) 'Growing together groups: working with parents and children from birth to three years of age', in M. Whalley and the Penn Green Team (eds), *Involving Parents in their Children's Learning*. London: Paul Chapman Publishing.

Tobin, J. (2005) 'Quality in early childhood education: an anthropologist's perspective', *Early Education and Development*, 16(4): 421–34.

Australian Association for Researchers in Education (AARE) (2013) *Ethical Guidelines*. Sydney: AARE.

Wengraf, T. (2001) *Qualitative Research Interviewing*. London: Sage.

Whalley, M. and the Pen Green Team (2007) *Involving Parents in their Children's Learning*. London: Paul Chapman Publishing.

CHAPTER 3

The value of practitioners being with children and parents together

Chapter overview

There is increasing international interest in practitioner-supported activities with parents and children together such as 'Supported Playgroups' in Australia and 'Stay and Plays' in England. These groups often have a dual-focus on early childhood education and/or parent support and more and more form part of government policy and models of integrated service provision internationally (Evangelou et al., 2007; Jackson, 2010; Needham, 2011; Parents as Partners in Early Learning, 2007). Dual-focused groups are facilitated by early childhood educators or other professional staff, with the main differences being related to the perceived purpose of the group. In this chapter we examine the ideological underpinnings of groups such as these and draw attention to the value and practical application of these types of service provision models. The importance of working together with families before their children start in formal early childhood settings such as pre-school or nursery is highlighted in this chapter, and we examine the benefits and challenges of working in this way. There is also a particular focus on parent and child well-being using the concepts of free encounter and parent peer support (Jackson, 2010; Vandenbroek et al., 2009b).

Stakeholders' perspectives

Central to effectively delivering dual-focused groups for parents and their children is the need to identify the motivations and purposes of the participating stakeholders: children, parents, practitioners, managers and funders. Building on Vygotsky's theory of how we learn socially through participating in activities with others, sociocultural research and analysis gives us further understanding about this type of work. It helps us understand how activities have developed over time and have evolved rules and tools to help make them work. We explore rules and tools in more detail in subsequent chapters but for the time being we concentrate on purpose.

Purpose is what motivates us to do something. One dimension of socio-cultural analysis is to explore the 'why' of people participating in activities with others. This sounds straightforward, but we often join in with activities when we are not quite sure what it is we are doing. People join a crowd to see what is going on; children join in household chores and might insist on taking hold of a broom to sweep the floor. They see that this activity involves moving the brush around, but they do not necessarily understand the adult's purpose is to collect dust into a pan and put it in the bin. With this in mind, if we are able to extend and share our understandings of purpose and participation, we are more likely to deliver effective dual-focused activities for parents and their children.

To put the above into a research context, when we are selecting settings or participants to study, preliminary exploration of people's objectives and aims is important. We need to check our understandings of what it is we are investigating and why. As researchers it is important to be open to the possibility that we may have labelled things incorrectly by mistaking one thing for another, thereby mixing two groups together. Or we may have seen things as separate when they are bound together, or failed to see that something has distinct and separate aspects. Consider the following two statements by group leaders:

> *Statement 1*
> This group is good in that parents are used to the routine and they do sit with their children and join in. Sometimes it is difficult to do this. We have talked about putting cushions out to encourage the parent to get down to the children's level. (Practitioner interview)

> *Statement 2*
> We are not involved in advising or educating, but the group does provide an environment for parents to share ideas about children's development. We predominantly encourage free play – encouraging children to play with their peers and not to be reliant on adult intervention to provide stimulation. (Practitioner questionnaire)

These contrasting statements from different group leaders illustrates a tension between parents and practitioners that commonly arises when the stated purpose of the group is to promote 'better interaction in play' but parents see the group as an opportunity to promote the growing independence of their children. These comments also reflect how different working practices can exist between people, even within the same group location.

By taking time to check the purpose of activities such as dual-focused groups (supporting parents and children) we are more likely to avoid what philosophers refer to as a 'category error'. Through exploration of stakeholders purposes we are able to focus on the intent behind parents and practitioners coming together to support children. We urge those working in such situations and researching into these environments that support children's early learning to critically examine the motivations of those participating by asking what it is they are aiming to achieve. In this chapter we compare the motives of some of the different stakeholders who have a say in what takes place in different activities involving parents. We wish to show how different motives may give rise to tensions between those participating in partnerships between professionals and parents.

Governments' purposes: evidence of the importance of parents and the home learning environment

Many governments around the world have demonstrated an increasing commitment to parent partnerships in early education in the past 20 years. In England, the New Labour government (2007–10) committed millions of pounds to develop Sure Start Local Programmes (SSLPs). This increasing commitment to supporting and working with parents was premised on emerging research on the impact that early education and parents have on children's later achievements, combined with the political capital of being seen to do something to support families and reduce child poverty (Needham, 2007).

Research data collected in the USA as part of the National Longitudinal Survey of Youth (NLSY) sampled the children of 12,686 women every two years from 1986 (Guo and Mullan-Harris, 2000). The data indicated that the most significant factor in predicting later achievement was 'cognitive stimulation in the home' which related to the availability of books and magazines, mothers reading to children, recorders being available and being taken on museum visits. This relates very closely to longitudinal research in the UK on a cohort of more than 2,000 children studied as part of the Effective Provision of Preschool Education (EPPE) (Sammons et al., 2007) that identified parental qualifications and the home learning environment (HLE) as far stronger influences on attainment than gender, socio-economic status, English as an additional language or free school meals. The EPPE study concluded that what parents do is more important than who they are (Sammons et al., 2002).

A similar longitudinal study of children's progress through the education system in New Zealand (Biddulph et al., 2003: 140) drew similar conclusions, suggesting that a family's influence on the child's educational achievement is not as clearly predicted by parents' socio-economic status as by family practices: 'Family processes which encourage positive interactions with others, and also provide a range of quality experiences and activities within and beyond the home enhance children's achievement. The influences of home processes are particularly evident in children's achievement in mathematics and literacy'.

As more government-funded activities with parents began, smaller, more qualitative and detailed studies were published which examined projects that worked with families in more depth. These also highlighted how much some families benefited from advice and support particularly in regard to the amount and quality of parent–child interactions (Weinberger et al., 2005).

Galboda-Liyanage et al. (2003) reported that their sample of 21 mothers, on average, classified and quantified their total joint activity with their children as 'play' 15 minutes, 'educational' 21 minutes and 'other' seven minutes on a particular day of study. These studies offer an insight into the variations in how mothers perceived they spent their time with their children.

In Australia, 'soft entry' activities such as supported playgroups are funded by the government within a prevention and early intervention policy framework. The aim is to increase opportunities for young children to engage in early childhood learning opportunities and to support parents through increased access to social support and other community networks. According to the New South Wales (NSW)[1] Department of Community Services (2009), the aim of prevention and early intervention strategies is to positively influence children's, parents' or families' behaviours in order to reduce the risk or ameliorate the effects of unfavourable social or physical environments. The goal of these strategies is to effect change so that protective factors outweigh risk factors and build resilience. It is argued that preventative programmes and interventions that offer social support to parents and quality learning environments to children, such as supported playgroups, are protective for families.

Thus for many governments the purpose of offering funding for promoting shared learning activity is about helping children to make a good start educationally and in particular about reducing inequality. That is, their intent is to help children from disadvantaged homes succeed by addressing challenging circumstances early, thus saving money in the long term.

THE VALUE OF PRACTITIONERS BEING WITH CHILDREN AND PARENTS TOGETHER

This might be considered a worthy aim but may give rise to problems because while parents are likely to share the purpose of wanting their children to make a good start in life, they are unlikely to want to be labelled or treated like failing parents. Labelling communities and the people that live within them as at risk or vulnerable is problematic and is the subject of a growing body of literature that critiques the prevailing prevention discourse (Carrington, 2002; France and Utting, 2005; Murray, 2004; Vandenbroeck et al., 2009b). However, while government funding continues to flow to early intervention and prevention activities, it is incumbent on those that implement them to explore and understand the meanings of these groups in the lives of those who participate in them (Jackson, 2010).

🔑 Key idea: a deficit model of parents' support

The evidence from larger-scale studies related to the lasting impact of the home learning environment has clearly been instrumental in garnering political interest in parental support. However, there is a danger when developing parenting interventions that some parents will be viewed as deficient in relation to interacting with children. A deficit model (Meighan and Siraj-Blatchford, 2003), similar to a medical model, labels a group as inherently deficient in some way compared with other groups. These models are rightly considered problematic when they fail to question whether the deficit is with the individual or with the situation that they are expected to fit into: 'society generates certain definitions of what the normal individual should be like, and those who fail to meet these definitions may become stigmatised' (Meighan and Siraj-Blatchford, 2003: 374).

Deficit models are also problematic in that they often present convenient labels that when applied to individuals lead to prejudiced stereotyped packages of support being offered. Further, deficit models often attribute problems to a single factor and ignore a range of other related contributing issues.

Nutbrown et al. (2005) identified the issue of deficit in regard to family literacy, suggesting that the term 'deficit approach' is not helpful because people need to recognise and acknowledge an area where they need to learn. 'Problems arise if differences (e.g. in literacy practices) are uncritically viewed as deficits, if deficits are imputed to learners without their assent, if deficits are exaggerated or if deficits are seen as all that learners have (i.e. their cultural strengths are devalued)' Nutbrown et al., 2005: 27).

In Australia, Biddulph et al. (2003) identify difference theory as an alternative to a deficit approach. This theory accepts the need to address the issue but does not locate the problem within the child or family. Rather it seeks to identify how institutionalised systems need to take more account of cultural heritage interacting with dominant discourses (Biddulph et al., 2003).

(Continues)

(Continued)

Bruner (2006) suggested that any deficit is not within the child or culture per se but that culture becomes part of the identity of the child very quickly. A potential deficit is created where the learning culture of schooling is not made equally accessible and transparent to those from different home-learning cultures. If educational outcomes such as the early acquisition of literacy and numeracy concepts remain as cornerstone targets for young children, and the means of acquiring these are controlled by books and styles of communication more suited to white middle-class children, then other sections of society will continue to be disadvantaged (Bruner, 2006). Evidence shows that to sustain parent and child participation it is important that professionals avoid creating a sense of deficit within the contexts in which they work with families (Parents as Partners in Early Learning, 2007; Weinberger et al., 2005; Whalley and the Pen Green Team, 2007).

Recommended further reading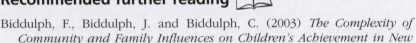

Biddulph, F., Biddulph, J. and Biddulph, C. (2003) *The Complexity of Community and Family Influences on Children's Achievement in New Zealand: Best Evidence Synthesis.* Wellington: Ministry of Education.

A moral and rights-based approach

In this book we are focusing on arguments that assert the rights of children and their parents to respect, dignity and equal opportunity to participate in society. We argue for a culture of parent partnerships based on a universal right to education in the broadest sense. We argue for education as the process that enables individuals' continued access to learning and personal development.

We believe that support for parents should, wherever possible, be framed in an egalitarian model because it is not just knowledge that is important but also the nature of the learning process. The learning process should promote positive attitudes to living and learning. It should promote learning as joyful, communal and playful, motivated by a desire to learn. In the remainder of this chapter we examine some of the evidence that illustrates not just that programmes of this sort are effective but why this might be so.

Professionals' purposes: cultures of practice in different countries – examples of supportive parent partnerships

There are many similarities between international service provision models in which parents and children participate jointly. Examples of these include: the Australian supported playgroup (Jackson, 2010), parent and toddler groups (Needham, 2011), Room to Play (Evangelou et al., 2006) and the Family Room (Whalley et al., 2007) in the UK; child and parent meeting places in Belgium (Vandenbroeck et al., 2009b), Italy (Musatti et al., 2009) and France (Service Petite Enfance, 2008); and the Norwegian Åpen Barnehage (open kindergarten) drop-in centres (Alvestad, 2009). All of these provide services for young children and parents together, and are led by early childhood educators or other professional staff. While there are also more parenting-skills-focused courses such as the Webster Stratton Programme, Parents as First Teachers (PAFT) and 'The Incredible Years' (Jackson and Needham, 2014), the following provides a discussion of dual-focused models that offer published and accessible evaluations of their approaches to working with parents and children jointly.

Australia

Supported playgroup provision in Australia is widespread and is outcomes focused. The model offers parents opportunities to meet and share their experiences, and offers children opportunities to play, learn and socialise. Supported playgroups are facilitated by early childhood teachers, community workers or allied health professionals with the aim of:

- stimulating children's development through quality early childhood experiences;
- increasing parental knowledge related to child development, early childhood learning and positive guidance skills;
- facilitating social networks;
- providing access to information and resources; and
- providing opportunities for the identification of developmental problems and referral to appropriate services.

The model is based substantially on evidence that emphasises that programmes that reduce parental social isolation through increased social support and provide children with stimulating play environments, promote children's positive developmental outcomes (Department of

Families, Housing, Community Services and Indigenous Affairs, 2009a; 2009b). Further, at the time of Jackson's (2010) study, implementation of supported playgroups was set within a political context in which the child protection system was being reformed in NSW (Wood, 2008). With extensive examination across the continuum of preventative, secondary and tertiary interventions, there is now a greater emphasis on universal strategies that provide preventative, family-focused support for vulnerable children and families (Higgins and Katz, 2008; Holzer et al., 2006; Wood, 2008). These strategies include the implementation of preventative models that reduce risk factors for neglect and maltreatment of children. Supported playgroups are considered one such model.

England

Parent and toddler groups such as Room to Play are widespread in England. An evaluative study conducted on Room to Play identifies similar benefits for parents and children to those found in the Australian evaluations, although there is a particular focus on prescribed curriculum content (Evangelou et al., 2006).

In relation to groups that involve parents learning with their children, there are a number of organisations in the UK that have led in developing thinking about the delivery of such shared learning groups. Pen Green, Thomas Coram and the Peers Early Education Partnership are examples where children's centres' own experience of provision has developed into training programmes and literature on working with parents (Evangelou et al., 2007; Pugh, 2002; Whalley and the Pen Green Team, 2007). These organisations have developed models where practitioners, parents and children stay together in sessions and are encouraged to share experiences and learn from each other. It is interesting to note that these organisations often focus relationship development around understanding the child's cognitive as well as social and emotional development, which was identified as being lacking in the organisation of some of the groups in an evaluation of children's centres in England (Anning et al., 2005). We have also drawn attention to the use of co-researching with parents, which is a feature of practice at Pen Green in Chapter 2.

This chapter has already drawn extensively from the limited literature related to working jointly alongside parents. The Peers Early Education Partnership (PEEP) is also one of the few programmes which has published a systematic evaluation of its impact on a community. The PEEP potentially offers scope for each of the categories derived from Epstein's model: parents as students in a lecture scenario, learning through osmosis in a play scenario, as understudies participating in professionally led activities, as partners in joint activity and as managers of a play scenario consulting professionals.

In PEEP parents retain primary responsibility, practitioners receive some training and guidance and the programme draws on the ORIM framework (Nutbrown et al., 2005). This framework encourages parents to reflect on how everyday occurrences provide:

- opportunities to develop key activities;
- recognise and celebrate children's achievements;
- interact, support, endorse and challenge; and
- model activities for children.

The PEEP project pays particular attention to pre-reading skills around story and rhyme sharing, but suggests applying the ORIM framework to a wider variety of activities supporting language and learning. PEEP began with a cluster of groups in Oxford and offered the two core elements of group time and home visiting. These were split into Early PEEP age groups (0–2s) and Foundation PEEP for children aged 3 and 4 (Evangelou et al., 2007; PEEP, 2008). PEEP's group sessions included Circle Time, Talking Time (discussion among parents), Story Time, Book Sharing, Borrowing Time and suggestions for games and activities to do at home.

Evaluations of the core PEEP groups (Evangelou et al., 2007) demonstrated that the PEEP programme made significant impacts on the rating of adult–child interactions and on a range of literacy skills. Evangelou et al. (2007) also identify an effect on a wider community space including those not attending sessions, suggesting the importance of outreach work, influence through pre-schools, schools and word of mouth. PEEP has been delivering training to groups involved in working with parents and young children since 2004 (PEEP, 2008).

The 'Share a learning' project run by ContinYou and funded by Department for Children Schools and Families (DCSF) was originally focused on schools offering activities for parents to try at home with their children. This project was extended to foundation stage classes in 2002 and was positively evaluated (Siraj-Blatchford and McCallum, 2004) with regard to the provision of quality materials for use at home to support learning. The evaluation suggested that children benefited greatly from being part of Share. Because the materials were good, children had fun, enhanced their learning and added to their play repertoire. 'Parents saw that Share had a positive impact on their children's basic and social skills, and on their disposition to learn' (Siraj-Blatchford and McCallum, 2004: 12). The report recommended more training for staff and the development of models that include children, parents and practitioners together in order to develop greater awareness of the style of conducting activities with children.

Professionals delivering dual-focused groups are faced with making difficult decisions on the balance of approaches to adopt: how much guidance to offer, how to offer guidance and whether to concentrate on supporting the parent or the child. The importance of offering support for parents' self-esteem, emotional well-being and bonding with their children are clearly important and connected issues (Jackson, 2006). The following chapters in this book will examine ways of addressing these various issues in more detail.

Parents' purposes

As we have already outlined, it is important to identify what parents are looking for when they bring their children to a shared learning group. Failing to recognise these purposes may lead to communication difficulties and a low take-up of the service offered. In the final section of this chapter we illustrate a parent's perspective.

Attendance at shared learning or dual-focused groups is entirely voluntary for most families, although some might be encouraged or compelled to attend by other professionals such as social workers. Grimshaw and Maguire (1998) identified that half of the parents they surveyed wanted to access a parenting programme before their child reached the age of three, although they also identified that parents needed programmes to be relevant to their own children and that parents adapted and modified what they received to fit their own perceived needs (Grimshaw and Maguire, 1998). The following exemplar vignette offers one parent's perspective on what attending a group with their child meant to them.

Case study: Liz, parent

It was June, winter had really set in and it was freezing cold. My sister said 'Come along to the playgroup, it's in the hall on Monday morning. It's great. There are lots of toys and there's morning tea.' I was hesitant to go because I didn't really feel like talking to anyone. I had just separated from my husband and I had moved my two young children from the city to be near my family.

I felt horrible, displaced, like being in a whirlwind. My whole world was upside down and I didn't know where to begin reforming my life. I was having a very hard time with my 22-month-old son who would not stop crying. He was not talking and was unable to communicate what was wrong. I didn't want to go to a playgroup and have others see how badly behaved my son was. I felt responsible for how he was turning out and felt like I was failing as a parent. I also had a 3-year-old daughter, however, who needed to play with other children, so I decided to go to playgroup.

I walked into the hall and felt at ease straight away. It was cheery and warm with puzzles, books, dolls houses, bikes, cars, blocks, slippery dips, painting and craft activities which were very inviting to children. There was also coffee, raisin toast and fruit which was very comforting for tired parents. I immediately felt welcomed by the women running the playgroup; I felt support but not threatened or judged. I could tell that the women were there to support me as a parent as much as they were there to support the children.

Every Monday I went to the playgroup to see people I now viewed as my friends. I felt the group kept me going throughout the week and I gained a lot of comfort from talking to other mothers and the staff. Slowly I started reaching out for help and telling others that I wasn't coping as a parent. As the weeks progressed my son was still crying a lot and unable to talk. He did not want to interact with others and was drawing away from me. I knew there was something wrong and I felt helpless.

One day at playgroup I saw an advertisement for early childhood developmental screening, so I discussed my concerns about my son with the facilitators. They arranged for a play-based assessment to be carried out with him during a playgroup session and I began to realise how useful this supported playgroup was to me. It had connected me with early childhood educators who had linked me to intervention specialists, speech and occupational therapists and other allied health professionals. I also had convenient access to a broad range of information and resources in one place.

I had found a great pathway where everyone linked up to provide the best service possible for my child. I did not have to do all of the running around to find the services; they were all talking to each other for the benefit of my child. Within a few months my son was formally diagnosed with high functioning autism and I realised that the playgroup had helped me receive support and access services easily when they were needed, not when it was too late.

This vignette was drawn directly from the transcript of a public talk that a mother gave about her experiences at an Australian playgroup. She gave permission for her story to be told as part of Jackson's (2010) research study and reiterated that joining the playgroup had been one of the best decisions she had ever made.

A major aim of the study from which this vignette is taken was to identify key attributes of effective supported playgroups that were successfully engaging families with young children (Jackson, 2010). Parent support emerged as a major component of all three groups with parents, facilitators and other stakeholders all reporting its significance. Importantly, the multifaceted nature of support in this context was evident throughout the data and eight categories emerged from the data analysis process which shed light on what research participants perceived and experienced as parent support: friendship and social network support; relational support; peer support; emotional support; parenting role support; information and resource support; 'circle of care' support and multidisciplinary support.

A similar in-depth study of 19 women in the UK explored the reasons why some women did not take up early interventions for their children (Barlow et al., 2004). The researchers outlined seven factors that influenced their choices; the women:

- did not agree with the professional who had referred them to the early intervention service;
- were not motivated by the way the service was presented;
- felt they had other more pressing needs;
- did not feel what was on offer was appropriate to their needs;
- did not feel comfortable sharing personal information with professionals; and
- felt they already had the support they needed from other formal or informal services.

The tensions identified by the women in this study may help to explain why there are many concerns about the take-up of early years services, particularly by families from disadvantaged groups with children aged under 3 years old. Smith et al. (2009) showed that although the take-up of free childcare places was high where information was carefully targeted, only 41 per cent of those surveyed used the other types of service offered by the delivery centres. This suggests that persuading many target families to participate in parent and toddler groups might be problematic, an issue which is developed further in the following sections.

The limited literature on parent and child shared provision suggests that this type of service is very popular with clients. From the perspective of existing users, the research also shows good levels of communication between parent and practitioner stakeholders. Following experience in peer consulting on the development of Sure Start services in Birmingham (UK) in the late 1990s, Wathall (2003) identified a number of parents that perceived the need for more parent and toddler provision. However, she also found a lack of information and awareness of what was actually available (Wathall, 2003). She writes that at the age of 37 as a first-time parent she found parenting very hard in terms of knowing what to do and coping physically and emotionally with her changed role and new isolation, despite attending an antenatal group and reading lots of information.

Similarly Anning et al. (2005) identified parents reporting that they valued practitioners who established positive, respectful relationships with them and their children. They valued services that provided opportunities for children to learn and socialise and services that enabled them to enjoy activities with their children. They preferred to access advice about parenting in a non-stigmatised setting and valued services giving them the chance to make friends. This enabled them to move on and set up their own networks of support.

Sure Start children's centre services in England have usually offered universal provision, that is, to anyone that wishes to access them, within a defined area. They are intended to be non-stigmatising services, therefore a range of parenting models are supported and this matches the type of provision many parents prefer (Anning et al., 2005). The models were intended to promote a positive self-image of parents as proactive and not reliant on professionals. The participation of a professional leader in such groups potentially offered greater scope to include vulnerable parents and to identify and support parenting needs in contrast to informal community-led groups. In practice, balancing different needs may sometimes be difficult to achieve and practitioners may have needed to juggle a range of parents' wishes for greater and lesser guidance (Wheeler and Connor, 2006).

Brooker (2002) compared teachers' and parents' perspectives on pedagogy as a group of children started in a school Reception class. She highlighted the differences between teacher's and some parent's attitudes to play in the curriculum. Brooker suggested that schools might do more to make their own pedagogic beliefs clear to parents and to find out more about parents' pedagogic beliefs. While Brooker's comments relate to induction into school, similar tensions between practitioners' and parents' perspectives are also visible in the writing of the Pen Green team. In relation to supporting parents in pre-school sessions Whalley and the Pen Green Team set out a model that includes effective pedagogical strategies:

> Staff at staff meetings extended their understanding of subtle intervention through discussion of Bruner's concept of 'scaffolding learning' (Bruner 1977), Vygotsky's Zone of Proximal development (Vygotsky, 1978) and Bruce's concept of 'match plus one' (Bruce, 1977). We shared the view with parents that an overzealous focus on teaching could inhibit the children's learning. What worked best for children was an approach that combined observation, subtle intervention and reflection. (Whalley and the Pen Green Team, 2007: 72)

Lareau (1997) presents a valuable insight into the nature of parent–school partnerships in the USA. Comparing two schools with contrasting middle-class and working-class catchment areas she draws attention to the comparatively less frequent and shorter spoken interactions between staff and parents in the working-class context. Lareau suggests that middle-class parents may have more flexibility and educational experience, enabling more comfortable connections with professional staff. Similarly, Reay (1998) also explored the differences in approach of 33 mothers from different social-class backgrounds supporting their children at two London primary schools. She pointed to a reciprocity between middle-class homes and primary schooling suggesting that the middle-class nature of schooling supports the cultural capital of middle-class homes to a greater extent than working-class homes and vice versa.

The three studies from Brooker, Lareau and Reay are helpful in identifying the space in which misalignments potentially occur between home and school cultures. These studies also alert us to the need to be inclusive in day-to-day practices. Dual-focused contexts are not necessarily the same as school situations because of the mixture of professionals facilitating the sessions. Therefore, class and role markers may be less in evidence in these contexts, particularly as services are targeted jointly at parents and children. The issue of bridging language and learning differences is an area that the study of dual-focused groups has the potential to illuminate. The development of parent and child learning groups represents the type of activity identified by both Lareau and Brooker which might help to inform parents and practitioners about the type of expectations that they each have. Groups represent an important opportunity to learn more about expectations of parental partnership, at a stage when educational subject knowledge is less important, and when relationships between parent and practitioner can be more equal.

 Reflective activities: developing a working culture

This chapter explored some of the evidence available in the literature that shows that shared learning activities in early education can make a significant impact on children's lives. We have also suggested that realising these benefits might be difficult to attain in practice. Developing positive trusting relationships with parents and carers is the key to achieving this and requires us to examine our own attitudes and the ways in which we consciously and subconsciously present ourselves.

1. Identify a time when you felt that your intentions were misunderstood. How did your actions contribute to that misunderstanding? Can you remember how that felt?
2. What steps could your team take to present itself to parents and practitioners? How could your team reflect on the way it is perceived by parents?
3. Reflect on what Liz, in this chapter's vignette, gained from her contact with the parent and child group. Consider how you might have responded to her.

Note

1. The state of New South Wales (NSW) is one of six states and two territories in Australia.

References

Alvestad, M. (2009) 'Early childhood education and care policy in Norway', *European Early Childhood Education Research Journal*, 17(3): 416–24.

Anning, A., Chesworth, E. and Spurling, L. (2005) *The Quality of Early Learning, Play and Childcare Services in Local Sure Start Programmes*. Nottingham: DfES Publications.

Barlow, J., Kirkpatrick, S., Stewart-Brown, S. and Davis, H. (2004) 'Hard to reach or out of reach? Reasons why women refuse to take part in early interventions', *Children and Society*, 19: 199–209.

Biddulph, F., Biddulph, J. and Biddulph, C. (2003) *The Complexity of Community and Family Influences on Children's Achievement in New Zealand: Best Evidence Synthesis*. Wellington: Ministry of Education.

Brooker, L. (2002) *Starting School: Young Children Learning Cultures*. Buckingham: Open University Press.

Bruner, J. (2006) 'Poverty and childhood', in J. Bruner (ed.), *In Search of Pedagogy*. Abingdon: Routledge. pp. 176–97.

Carrington, V. (2002) *New Times: New Families*. Dordrecht: Kluwer Academic.

Department of Families, Housing, Community Services and Indigenous Affairs (2009) 'Playgroups', accessed 1 November 2009 at www.fahcsia.gov.au/internet/facsinternet.nsf/family/parenting-playgroups.htm.

Evangelou, M., Smith, S. and Sylva, K. (2006) *Evaluation of the Sutton Trust shopping centre project: Room to play*. Oxford: University of Oxford Department of Educational Studies.

France, A. and Utting, D. (2005) 'The paradigm of "risk and protection-focused prevention" and its impact on services for children and families', *Children and Society*, 19: 77–90.

Galboda-Liyanage, K.C., Scott, S. and Prince, M.J. (2003) 'Time budgets of the mothers of pre-school children: an analysis of mother child joint activities', *British Journal of Developmental Psychology*, 21: 273–83.

Grimshaw, R. and Maguire, C. (1998) *Evaluating Parenting Programmes: A Study of Stakeholders' Views*. York: Joseph Rowntree Foundation.

Guo, G. and Mullan-Harris, K. (2000) 'The mechanisms mediating the effects of poverty on children's intellectual development', *Demography*, 37(4): 431–47.

Higgins, D. and Katz, I. (2008) 'Enhancing service systems for protecting children', *Family Matters*, 80: 43–51.

Holzer, P., Higgins, J., Bromfield, L., Richardson, N. and Higgins, D. (2006)

'The effectiveness of parent education and home visiting child maltreatment prevention programs', *Child Abuse Prevention Issues*, 24: 1–23.

Jackson, D. (2006) 'Playgroups as protective environments for refugee children at risk of trauma', *Australian Journal of Early Childhood*, 31(2): 1–5.

Jackson, D. (2010) *A Place to 'be': Supported Playgroups a Model of Relational, Social Support for Parents and Children*. [online], University of Western Sydney.

Jackson, D. and Needham, M. (2014) 'It ain't what you do, it's the way that you do it!', in M. Reed and R. Walker (eds), *Early Childhood Studies: A Critical Companion*. London: Sage.

Lareau, A. (1997) 'Social-class differences in family-school relationships: the importance of cultural capital', in A.H. Halsey, H. Lauder, P. Brown, and A. Stuart Wells (eds), *Education Culture, Economy and Society*. Oxford: Oxford University Press. pp. 707–17.

Meighan, R. and Siraj-Blatchford, I. (2003) *A Sociology of Educating*. London: Continuum.

Murray, K. (2004) 'Do not disturb: "Vulnerable populations" in federal government policy discourses and practices', *Canadian Journal of Urban Research*, 13(1): 50–69.

Musatti, T., Picchio, M. and Scopelliti, M. (2009) 'Parents' perception of their toddler's needs for socialization', paper presented at the 19th European Early Childhood Education Research Association annual conference, Strasbourg, 26–29 August.

Needham, M. (2007) 'Keeping people in the big picture: national policy and local solutions', in I. Siraj-Blatchford, K. Clarke and M. Needham (eds), *The Team Around the Child*. Stoke: Trentham.

Needham, M. (2011) *Learning to Learn in Supported Parent and Toddler Groups: A Sociocultural Investigation*. [online], London University.

Nutbrown, C., Hannon, P. and Morgan, A. (2005) *Early Literacy Work with Families*. London: Sage.

Parents as Partners in Early Learning (2007) *Parental Involvement – a Snapshot of Policy and Practice*. London: DCSF.

Peers Early Education Programme (PEEP) (2008) *PEEP Practitioner Manual*. Oxford: Peers Early Education Project.

Pugh, G. (2002) *Contemporary Issues in the Early Years*. London: Paul Chapman Publishing.

Reay, D. (1998) *Class Work; Mother's Involvement in their Children's Primary Schooling*. London: UCL Press.

Sammons, P., Sylva, K., Melhuish, E., Siraj-Blatchford, I., Taggart, B. and Elliot, K. (2002) *Technical Paper 8a: Measuring the Impact of Pre-School on Children's Cognitive Progress Over the Pre-School Period*. London: Institute of Education.

Sammons, P., Sylva, K., Melhuish, E., Siraj-Blatchford, I., Taggart, B. and Grabbe, Y. (2007) *Influences on Children's Attainment and Progress in Key Stage 2: Cognitive Outcomes in Year 5*. London: Institute of Education.

Service Petite Enfance (2008) *Projet enfants/parents ensemble*. Illkirch-Graffenstaden, Strasbourg: Ville d'Illkirch-Graffenstaden.

Siraj-Blatchford, I. and McCallum, B. (2004) *An Evaluation of Share at the Foundation Stage*. London: University of London, Institute of Education.

Smith, R., Purdon, S., La Valle, I., Wollny, I. Owen, R. et al. (2009) *Early Education Pilot for Two Year Old Children Evaluation*. London: National Centre for Social Research.

Vandenbroeck, M., Roets, G. and Snoeck, A. (2009a) 'Immigrant mothers crossing borders: nomadic identities and multiple belongings in early childhood education', *European Early Childhood Education Research Journal*, 17(2): 203–16.

Vandenbroeck, M., Boonaert, T., Van Der Mespel, S. and De Brabandere, K. (2009b) 'Dialogical spaces to reconceptualize parent support in the social investment state', *Contemporary Issues in Early Childhood*, 10(1): 66–77.

Wathall, S. (2003) 'Sure start making a difference? A parents perspective', in J. Kai and C. Drinkwater (eds), *Primary Care in Urban Disadvantaged Communities*. Oxford: Radcliffe Medical Press.

Weinberger, J., Pickstone, C. and Hannon, P. (2005) *Learning from Sure Start*. Maidenhead: Open University Press.

Whalley, M. and the Pen Green Team (2007) *Involving Parents in their Children's Learning*. London: Paul Chapman Publishing.

Wheeler, H. and Connor, J. (2006) *Parents, Early Years and Learning; A Reader*. London: National Children's Bureau.

Wood, J. (2008) *Report of the Special Commission of Inquiry into Child Protection Services in NSW*. Sydney: State of NSW.

PART 2

A PLACE TO BE AND A SPACE TO GROW

CHAPTER 4

Being together as parents

Chapter overview

Internationally informal early childhood settings are being used to bring parents together in mutually supportive ways. In this chapter the Australian supported playgroup is discussed as an example of a dual-focused setting that provides a responsive, social space for parents and children to be together. Drawing on research into the supported playgroup model (Jackson, 2011), the chapter shows how this type of early years' service can assist in the reduction of social isolation and contribute to parents' sense of well-being, confidence and ability to support one another, particularly in relation to being a parent. Eight categories of parent support within the supported playgroup context are described and parent perspectives are presented to illustrate how parents of young children appreciate being able to come to a place where they can 'be'. The chapter also discusses challenges relating to the professional facilitator's role and the need to sometimes balance the dual purposes of the playgroups, that is, adult social interaction and parent–child interaction. The chapter concludes with a discussion focused on the complex and debated notion of parent support. It is proposed that groups such as supported playgroups demonstrate a model of bringing parents and children together where value is placed on each parent's role within their family, regardless of circumstance.

Introduction

As outlined in Chapter 3, there are a number of different dual-focused models operating internationally that support parents and their children together. The Australian supported playgroup is one such model which became the subject of my doctoral research study (Jackson, 2010). This chapter uses this study to draw attention to the ways in which bringing parents together in this type of service can provide support and assist the development of their children.

Supported playgroups are informal and sessional. Parents and their young children come together with a facilitator to socialise and share their experiences while their children engage in play-based early childhood activities. Their widespread use across Australia demanded informed understandings of the influence of these types of groups in the lives of children and their parents and led to my case study research that identified key attributes of three effective supported playgroups. One of the outcomes of the study was the identification of eight categories of parent support. These categories assist in moving our knowledge away from vague or suspected ideas of support, towards descriptions that capture the essence of what participants in supported playgroups or similar models experience and articulate as parent support. These categories provide valuable insights for practitioners providing dual-focused groups and for others whose interests lie in providing and monitoring supportive, social spaces for parents and their children.

It is important to note before describing the categories that dual-focused groups such as this have the potential to support all parents, not just those who are known to be experiencing vulnerabilities because of their circumstances. The research discussed here suggests that parenting is experienced along a continuum where all parents have the potential to demonstrate their capacities and strengths but also to experience the need for support in their roles. It also suggests that the journey back and forth along this continuum occurs regardless of a family's formation, social or economic status, or classification within a government funding framework.

Categories of parent support

Friendship and social network support

Friendships and the formation of social networks that reduce social isolation are important sources of support for parents participating in dual-focused groups and are integral to what parents experience as supportive. Facilitated groups such as these have the potential to support positive interactions with and between *all* families. This is true regardless of whether families are perceived to be vulnerable or well functioning as is often the case in targeted, government-funded programmes.

Parents in my study spoke at length about being able to come to a place where they could 'be themselves and chat' and about the value of making new friends and sharing common experiences related to raising children. Numerous examples were given that illustrated the support that they experienced through their friendships both with other parents and the facilitators. 'I don't know what I would do without playgroup' was also a comment made on many occasions, and some parents offered further explanations which highlighted the importance of the connections they made within these groups, and their effect on their well-being and the ultimate well-being of their children:

Case study

I wouldn't have any friends with babies if it wasn't for [playgroup] … [playgroup] has like saved S's [child's] life. And also, not so much my life, but definitely saved S's life. If I hadn't gone to [playgroup] … it was bad. Actually [playgroup] probably didn't save S's life, I probably did because I got myself involved with [child protection agency]. But going to [playgroup] and seeing all the other mums and watching how they interact with their children as well and seeing all the other kids and S was able to play with other kids her age, it was so much of a saviour … I don't know what I would've done if I hadn't gone to [playgroup] … that's what me and S looked forward to every week … Yeah, if I hadn't gone to [playgroup] and gotten involved with other parents and other children, S would have probably gone to someone else long ago. Like now she's with my mum, which I am happy about, but she would've been fostered out which I would have hated. So it's so much [playgroup] saved us.   (Young parent)

The friendships that they make, I think, is the most important aspect … when you look at all of that happen, and I think as workers, if we can set that up and set the forum up for them to meet in a safe space and be there if they need us, is fantastic, because they can do the rest …   (Facilitator)

To add to this, many parents reported that they now participated in broader community activities and had increased their social networks and become more linked to their local school or community as a result of their playgroup attendance:

It [playgroup] might hold mums together … and keeps communities closer-knit, or strengthens the bonds in a community so people can help each other a bit more because they know each other a bit better.

(Continues)

(Continued)

> It's probably not something you can really quantify … I walk around the community and I'm like, hello, hello and I know lots and lots of people and I can see him [partner] going, you seem to know everyone around here. And how valuable is that? How do you quantify or put a value on that, the fact that you can walk around in your own community and know people?   (Parent)

Allowing time for parents to socialise within these types of groups, however, also presents challenges to facilitators and sometimes to other group members. As dual-focused groups have the purpose of providing opportunities for parents to interact with their children as well as with each other, tensions arise around striking a balance between these dual purposes:

> The parents I think get a lot out of spending time with each other. That is always a dilemma because I think, for some of them, it's life-saving but that means they don't spend much time with their children so it's kind of how you mediate between those two things … (Facilitator)

To address the challenges of balancing this dual purpose there needs to be ongoing consideration of the context and particular needs of the group. The groups focus needs to be structured responsively to reflect these understandings.

Relational support

The tension described above was also addressed by some group facilitators through a process of mediation which both assisted each participant to see others' perspectives and supported the maintenance and further development of positive relationships within the group. Managing group dynamics was an important aspect of the support provided to parents and although this was challenging, facilitators reflected on and addressed any tensions that arose through action that supported the further development of positive relationships within the groups.

This assistance in enhancing the social connectedness between families, in turn promoted parents' continued participation, increased their access to support and reduced social isolation. These are all factors which are known to be protective for children (Ghate and Hazel, 2002; Vandenbroeck et al., 2009).

There's always the risk that people will come and actually be harmed because the interactions are negative towards them, and they actually go away feeling less well off than when they came. So because of that risk, I think it's quite important to keep an eye on the overall dynamic, and make sure that that stays positive and moves towards consciously demonstrating strength-based parenting … it's how you deal with your own feelings about seeing parenting you're not that comfortable with … and it's good to just have support for the feelings you're having, but have some other ways to manage the interactions with that parent. Because as you know, if you are doing the wrong thing, if you feel judged as well, it doesn't really help you change. It just makes you feel more (probably) bad about yourself, which might be where the problem's coming from in the first place. (Facilitator)

Peer support

Peer support is an important element in dual-focused groups because it increases parents' ability to learn from each other. Through observing their children's interactions with other children and adults and discussing relevant issues with their peers, parents are able to gain new knowledge and perspectives that promote their confidence in parenting.

R: So do you have any new knowledge or insights as a result of attending the playgroup?
X: My understanding of myself as a parent and of other people's skills as parents.
Y: You do pick up things, like if your child is going through something you can talk to other parents and get more of an idea of what to do.
P: Yes, and you can see that everybody has different styles of parenting. It's OK.
X: I know myself you come in and think it should be like this and gradually you see it works for them and it works for me, each to their own and it has helped me very much with child rearing and learning to relax.
P: And how every parent handles different childhood situations and it's been really good because I've probably got the most children, like I'm a mother of four and I know I'm one of the parents with the oldest children and I had my set ways of how you must parent because of how I was brought up. I see how other parents do it and I know that won't exactly work for my child but I can adapt that to work for my child because every child is so different and you have to approach them differently. You get ideas on how to approach your child just from watching other parents and from information that [the facilitator] has brought in or other organisations have brought in.
X: There's been practical learnings, just simple things that you couldn't measure in a book … you are subconsciously assimilating a lot … (Researcher [R] and focus group parents [X,Y,P])

Emotional support

Emotional support is integral to the relationships developed by group facilitators with parents, particularly in cases where parents are known not to have experienced nurturing relationships themselves. Parents benefit greatly from facilitators who express genuine care and respect for them and appreciate being listened to. It is important to them to develop relationships with facilitators that are based on mutual respect, understanding and care and this type of support enhances their ability to provide nurturing care to their children.

> This is going to sound stupid, but the cups of tea. I used to come in; I didn't sleep like the first eight months that my babies were alive … And I'd come in, and I'd be like, I'm exhausted. And she'd meet me at the door, and she'd meet me at the car sometimes, and take my babies off me, and hand them out to people and make me a cup of tea … it was so nice. And I'd just sit there and drink a cup of tea, and go, oh my goodness, I'm going to die … the amount of times that I've had a cry … I used to come in and I'd be not sleeping for days, and I'd be going mad. She'd say, 'You know what? You're doing it on your own, you've been sleepless, you're breast feeding, you've got a house to take care of and three children, what do you expect from yourself? It's too much for one person. And then I'd be like, you know what, I'm a legend … (Young parent of a 4-year-old and 2-year-old twins)

Parenting role support

Dual-focused groups have the potential to be non-judgmental spaces in which parents feel supported in their parenting role. In order for this to occur facilitators of these groups must respect parents as the most important people in their children's lives and be diligent in their efforts to listen to their views and affirm their roles. They also need to model behaviours and provide gentle guidance related to child development and parental expectations. Groups such as these can provide opportunities for parents to gain new insights and to co-construct new skills about parenting which are reflected in positive changes in their relationships with their children:

> I guess I do a bit of positive stuff about what a great job they're doing, you have to be a bit careful not to patronise … I think anything that makes somebody feel better about themselves and about the world helps them to be a better parent so I think that's really important. People come away from that group saying 'Oh, someone really listened to me today and someone thought that was such an amazing thing I've been doing' so of course that is going to make them a better parent. I think that you can get all the information you like out of a book or a course about what to do but if that doesn't change who you are then, it's the things that change your view of yourself and how you view the world, they are the things that change who you are as a parent and that can happen when you are just in a space where you are appreciated and where you get to talk about yourself. (Facilitator)

I think just watching how the things that the workers do with the kids, and watching what they're ... the interactions that they have with the kids gives you ideas on what you can do at home with the kids. Whereas normally you just go, Oh go away, I've had enough of you. Go away. (Young parent)

I'm more patient with my children. I grew up in that sort of family where you hit first and ask questions about the problem later, whereas now I'm basically learning to find out more about what's happened before I instantly say 'oh, it's your fault' ... From watching another parent and also from [the facilitator], things she's brought in and just talking to people ... (Parent)

Information and resource support

The provision of practical, timely support assists parents in groups to address issues that are pressing for them at the time. If facilitators' have a broad knowledge of local services and combine this with their knowledge of child development, it enables them to support parents at a time and place that is appropriate and relevant to them:

I remember there was one time, B threw an absolute wobbly [tantrum] in the toilet there and one of the staff came because I was struggling to know what to do ... one of the staff came and she said something or suggested a book I could read, or something like that. And it just made me realise that there was a different way of handling that situation than the one I was using. Which was obviously not working anyway. (Parent)

The same parent described her playgroup as a 'hub' for information and likened providing timely support to parents to teaching children to read:

It just makes sense to me. It's like reading. Do you read to them from birth, a little bit at a time, or do you wait till they go to school and then start reading to your children? Do you support mums and families from the very beginning, or do you wait until the wheels are falling off? (Parent)

'Circle of care' support

The diverse needs of families within these dual-focused groups can also be addressed by a broader network of practitioners. This 'circle of care' which in some instances may include informal case work, enables a more knowledgeable and holistic approach to meeting individual needs. Parents benefit from this 'one-stop shop' experience which provides them with emotional and practical support and builds their capacity for ongoing participation in the groups.

For example, in one of the groups studied there was a level of 'behind the scenes' discussion that took place between the facilitator and other professionals that ensured that the needs and vulnerabilities of particular parents were addressed. These discussions only took place with the parent's permission and within the policy frameworks relating to confidentiality within the organisations involved. The facilitator in this group described one occasion in which a professional from another group contacted her to tell her that a mother with severe depression would be attending her playgroup. It was explained that the mother really needed extra support because of her mental illness so, with this awareness, the facilitator built a trusting relationship with the mother. In time the mother chose to share the nature of her depression with the facilitator and her playgroup peers and this 'circle of care' contributed to her ongoing engagement in the group.

Multidisciplinary support

Dual-focused groups can also act as a platform for multidisciplinary support that enables families to access resources and support within non-clinical, non-stigmatising, universal environments. Practitioners from a range of disciplines, such as health, welfare and early childhood intervention, are able to gently embed more formal types of support within these contexts and this assists parents in ways that might otherwise be unavailable to them.

> I had found a great pathway [at playgroup] where everyone linked up to provide the best service possible for my child. I did not have to do all of the running around to find the services; they were all talking to each other for the benefit of my child. Within a few months my son was formally diagnosed with high functioning autism and I realised that the playgroup had helped me receive support and access services easily when they were needed, not when it was too late.   (Parent)

Each of the categories described above is a significant component of support in its own right. When found in combination they contribute to social spaces that provide optimal, multidimensional and identifiable support to all parents.

Notions of parent support

Parent support is a complex and debated notion to which multiple meanings are attached. There is extensive debate about the construct of parenting and support (see for example Clarke, 2006; Gillies, 2005a,

2005b, 2006; Vandenbroeck et al., 2009), and the examples given above provide a significant insight into what some parents with young children find supportive within dual-focused service contexts.

The strength of the supported playgroups in my study was their ability to bring parents and children together and to place value on each parent's role within their family, regardless of circumstance. Importantly, each group provided social support and access to information and resources that were defined and driven by parents and accessed at a time and place that they determined. The type of social, semi-formal support that these types of groups offer parents reflects what the literature reports is most wanted by and protective for parents, and what is most lacking in many formal parenting programmes (Quinton, 2004; Rullo and Musatti, 2005; Vandenbroeck et al., 2009).

Further, all the manifestations of parent support identified above are underpinned by genuine relationships through which knowledge is co-constructed rather than 'delivered by an expert'. A facilitated partnership approach where parents can 'be' enables new understandings about parenting to be socially constructed among parents and practitioners.

🔑 Key idea: pedagogicalising parenting

A growing number of authors argue that programmes that aim to 'support' parents of young children, often 'pedagogicalise' parenting by implementing strategies that aim to teach parents how to parent (Gewirtz, 2001; Gillies, 2005a; Vandenbroeck et al., 2009). These authors view the increasing worldwide trend to implement formal parenting programmes as an attempt to inculcate middle-class values at the family level. They criticise the enforcing of middle-class constructs of parenting as a means of shifting blame to parents rather than addressing systemic social problems such as poverty and its associated effects on family health and well-being. Further, they suggest that policies that focus on universalising an 'expert' view of parenting perpetuate the assumption that parents who do not 'parent' in particular ways provide inadequate support for their children's learning and development.

In contrast, the types of interaction described earlier in this chapter between parents and practitioners, reflect the Vygotskian notion of socially constructed learning (Vygotsky, 1978). These types of environments encourage parents to share their experiences of parenting with one another and enable them to be 'scaffolded' by facilitators if needed. What is important in these interactions is that the search for new knowledge is instigated by parents, rather than directed by facilitators within a predetermined curriculum framework, or on the basis of an 'expert' belief about what what parents need. Practitioners need to work in partnership with parents

(Continues)

(Continued)

to co-construct ways of being a parent within contextual circumstances, rather than constructing ways to teach parenting.

Following on from this, facilitators in my study held the belief that they should create environments for parents to 'be' and that their relationships with parents should be built on a belief in parents' capacities to parent. This is not to say that many participants in their groups did not have other issues that interfered with their ability to parent, for example, mental health issues or drug and alcohol abuse, but that *these* were the main issues that they needed help in addressing; the issue was not parenthood. The groups were characterised by practitioners working relationally alongside parents rather than imposing a deficit, problematised programme format that a number of authors argue against (Gillies, 2005a; Vandenbroeck et al., 2009).

Recommended further reading

Vandenbroeck, M., Boonaert, T., Van Der Mespel, S. and De Brabandere, K. (2009) 'Dialogical spaces to reconceptualize parent support in the social investment state', *Contemporary Issues in Early Childhood*, 10(1): 66–77.

It is important that practitioners in dual-focused groups maintain a relationship focus in their work with parents that draws on a strengths-based practice framework. Practitioners need to interact with parents in ways that suggest they believe that parents have tacit parenting knowledge and which demonstrate their willingness to work alongside parents to create environments that maximise their strengths and abilities. In the same way that early childhood educators create relational environments that foster children's abilities to develop, dual-focused groups should be environments in which parents can develop beside nurturing facilitators who understand and recognise the strengths that lay within them.

The role of dual-focused groups to nurture parents is supported in the research of numerous authors who articulate that nurturing relationships greatly affect adults' positive feelings about parenthood. They reiterate that these relationships allow parents to shape their lives, while allowing practitioners to provide instruction and encouragement for change as it is needed (Munford and Sanders, 2006).

Evidence from Swick et al. (2001) also shows that it is through ongoing, nurturing interactions with their parents that children's emotional development is fostered. Children who experience loving relationships and empathetic interactions learn how to care and be nurturing themselves. This developmental pathway is described eloquently by Elshtain (1999: 18), who says that as humans we are 'talked into talking and loved into loving'.

Munford and Sanders (2006) concur with this view but point to the critical need for parents to have experienced nurturing relationships themselves in order to provide them for their children. They argue that formal skills-based parenting instruction does not in itself develop the ability to nurture.

Prioritising time for all parents to feel nurtured is a vital dimension of service provision. Given the evidence that in any dual-focused group there may often be many parents who have not experienced the relationships described above, the nurturing support they receive may make them more able to provide nurturing interactions and environments for their children, thus fostering their emotional development.

Arguably the support that practitioners provide through mediation of adult relationships is also a component of nurture within this type of setting. Positive relationships between participants is vital to the outcomes described earlier, however, negative interactions may threaten these relationships and mediation is an appropriate intervention. Berry and Letendre (2004) contend that it is beneficial for parents to participate in social programmes where facilitators are prepared to address relationship issues as they occur within the group dynamic. Attention to adult relationship skills, they argue, leads to more durable gains in parenting skills.

There are growing concerns raised in the literature related to parenting programmes that are delivered within the prevailing prevention climate. Vandenbroeck et al. (2009) and others argue that prevention programmes by their nature aim to intervene before problems arise, based on a probable assumption that in the presence of certain risk factors problems will occur in the future. Programmes delivered under such circumstances have the potential to confirm existing stereotypes of families and perpetuate the underlying assumption that being a parent is a risk factor in itself (Gillies, 2005a, 2005b; Vandenbroeck et al., 2009).

For example, in my study there was a programme that was funded to target parents who were at risk because of multiple factors (including young parenthood) but where there were a number of parents whom facilitators described as doing well regardless of their risk factors. These parents, along with the rest of the parents in the group, could have felt further marginalised if they perceived that facilitators thought that they needed to be 'taught' how to parent. This did not happen, however, because the playgroup provided a non-stigmatising, social environment in which intervention related to parenting skills took place at parents' discretion, within a system of trusting relationships that did not presume they were 'empty vessels'.

The friendships and social networks that parents develop in these dual-focused environments are also integral to the parents' experiences of support. The amount of data related to friendship in my study illustrated the extent to which these types of groups can provide an accepting and welcoming environment that builds bonding social capital (Leonard and

Onyx, 2004). Many parents reported that they participated in broader community activities as a direct result of attending the playgroups over an extensive period of time, which demonstrated the model's ability to also act as a catalyst for the formation of bridging social capital (Leonard and Onyx, 2004). Most importantly though, the social networks that the playgroups provided supported the well-being of parents, which is known to increase positive outcomes for children, especially those exposed to high-risk or neglectful environments (Barnes et al., 2006).

Finally, the ability to provide multidisciplinary support at a time and place that suits families is a crucial element of this type of early years setting. Genuine relationships developed between parents and practitioners provide opportunities for more formal types of interventions to occur. These can often take place within the universal, non-stigmatising environments of the groups rather than in clinical settings which can be a barrier to engagement, particularly for isolated families.

Significantly in my study there were families who may not have made contact with the formal supports that they needed if their access had not been supported through the substantive relationships that they developed within the playgroups. This reflects the wider evidence which suggests that successful early intervention programmes are often community based and integrate the contributions of multiple disciplines to coordinate supports and services based on family needs (Barnes et al., 2006; Shonkoff and Phillips, 2000).

Dual-focused groups can offer parents a 'soft entry' place that is able to meet their need for social interaction and help them engage with formal supports when necessary. The ability of these groups to provide access to information and resources and to link families successfully to other relevant support services is also significant as it makes it more likely that these families will feel confident to engage with and trust other services in the future (Ghate and Hazel, 2002). Given that families experiencing vulnerability are often and somewhat problematically described as 'hard to reach' and are most unlikely to take up formal supports (Ghate and Hazel, 2002; Sylva et al., 2004), dual-focused groups provide a unique mechanism that potentially helps families to negotiate and engage with the formal service system.

We can see by the examples given in this chapter that it is possible to facilitate social environments for parents which focus on and encourage support through mutual sharing and reciprocity. Dual-focused groups hold the potential to decrease parents' social isolation, increase parents' confidence and increase access to formal support services, all of which are known to promote positive developmental outcomes for children. The nature of the peer support and learning that parents can experience in this type of service model demonstrates the true value of providing safe, social spaces that allow parents to 'be'.

Reflective activities: dual-focused models

In this chapter Australian supported playgroups were discussed as an example of responsive, social spaces that enhance parent and child well-being and eight categories of parent support were outlined. Dual-focused groups were presented as a service model that has the potential to assist in the reduction of social isolation and contribute to parents' sense of well-being, confidence and ability to support one another, particularly in relation to being a parent.

1. Using the eight categories of parent support, identify three ways in which you could create an environment that is supportive for parents.
2. Imagine you are the facilitator in a dual-focused group for parents with young children. What strategies would you use to promote co-constructive learning between practitioners and parents?
3. This chapter has described the importance of nurturing relationships with parents. How would you incorporate this aspect of parent support in a dual-focused group that has an intentional focus on children's literacy?

References

Barnes, J., Katz, I., Korbin, J.E. and O'Brien, M. (2006) *Children and Families in Communities: Theory, Research, Policy and Practice.* Chichester: John Wiley and Sons.

Berry, M. and Letendre, J. (2004) 'Lambs and lions: the role of psychoeducational groups in enhancing relationship skills and social networks', *Groupwork*, 14(1): 30–45.

Clarke, K. (2006) 'Childhood, parenting and early intervention: a critical examination of the Sure Start national programme', *Critical Social Policy*, 26(4): 699–721.

Elshtain, J. (1999) 'A call to civil society', *Society*, 36(5): 11–19.

Gewirtz, S. (2001) 'Cloning the Blairs: New Labour's programme for the re-socialization of working-class parents', *Journal of Education Policy*, 16(4): 365–78.

Ghate, D. and Hazel, N. (2002) *Parenting in Poor Environments. Stress, Support and Coping.* London: Policy Research Bureau.

Gillies, V. (2005a) 'Meeting parents' needs? Discourses of "support" and "inclusion" in family policy', *Critical Social Policy*, 25(1): 70–90.

Gillies, V. (2005b) 'Raising the "Meritocracy": parenting and the individual-ization of social class', *Sociology*, 39(5): 835–53.

Gillies, V. (2006) 'Working class mothers and school life: Exploring the role of emotional capital', *Gender and Education*, 18(3): 281–93.

Jackson, D. (2011) 'What's really going on? Parents' views of parent support in three Australian supported playgroups', *Australian Journal of Early Childhood*, 36(4): 29–37.

Leonard, R. and Onyx, J. (2004) *Social Capital and Community Building Spinning Straw into Gold*. London: Janus.

Munford, R. and Sanders, J. (2006) *Strengths-based Social Work with Families*. Melbourne: Thomson.

Quinton, D. (2004) *Supporting Parents: Messages from the Research*. London: Jessica Kingsley.

Rullo, G. and Musatti, T. (2005) 'Mothering young children: child care, stress and social life', *European Journal of Psychology of Education*, 20(2): 107–19.

Shonkoff, J. and Phillips, D. (2000) *From Neurons to Neighborhoods*. Washington, DC: National Academy Press.

Swick, K., Da Ros, D. and Kovach, B. (2001) 'Empowering parents and families through a caring inquiry approach', *Early Childhood Education Journal*, 29(1): 114–17.

Sylva, K., Melhuish, E.C., Sammons, P., Siraj-Blatchford, I. and Taggart, B. (2004) *Effective Pre-school Provision*. London: Institute of Education.

Vandenbroeck, M., Boonaert, T., Van Der Mespel, S. and De Brabandere, K. (2009) 'Dialogical spaces to reconceptualize parent support in the social investment state', *Contemporary Issues in Early Childhood*, 10(1): 66–77.

Vygotsky, L.S. (1978) *Mind in Society: The Development of Higher Psychological Processes*. Cambridge, MA: Harvard University Press.

CHAPTER 5

Creating a nurturing community

Chapter overview

The widespread use of dual-focused models calls for considerable attention to be paid to the nature of facilitation in this type of service provision. This is particularly important when practitioners are working in settings where families are experiencing multiple vulnerabilities. This chapter discusses the critical role of facilitation in dual-focused groups and again uses examples from the Australian-supported playgroup research referred to in previous chapters (Jackson, 2010). It will demonstrate how the engagement and on-going participation of diverse families in this type of service provision reflects the satisfaction and support that they experience. Importantly, it will highlight that this satisfaction and support is directly related to the role that facilitators play in creating accepting and responsive environments for families.

The role that facilitators play in creating engaging and supportive dual-focused environments is inextricably tied to the support that parents experience. Congruent with the various forms of parent support described in the previous chapter, the functions of facilitation is this type of service provision is multidimensional and complex. In my research (Jackson,

2010) I identified four categories that shed light on these functions and their relationship to family engagement and participation:

- family-centred practice – focusing on parents and children;
- the care factor – trust and engagement;
- creating a 'space'; and
- knowledge of the local service system – access to other information and resources.

This chapter explores these categories and uses them to shed light on the role of the facilitator in dual-focused contexts such as supported playgroups.

Across the sites that I studied, participants were asked to describe the characteristics of a successful facilitator. There was considerable consistency in responses from parents, facilitators and principals at the schools where two of the groups operated. They spoke at length about the knowledge, skills and attitudes that were critical to effective facilitation:

> There's a lot of qualities, really. Someone who's open, who's non-judgmental, who's actually quite skilled in communication, all sorts of communication, not just verbal, non-verbal as well. Who has a knowledge of community services, and who can, off the top of their heads, either refer straight away, or know where to get information to refer. Someone who is also good with kids, who has early childhood education expertise. Because often a parent will want you to check out the child, in term of its language development, or whatever. And it's also pretty crucial to observe kids, and just to have a general understanding of early childhood development. (Facilitator)

> The ability to listen ... professionalism, someone who's confidential.
> Persistence, I reckon it was a really good trait that [the facilitator] had ... and she was calm and was easy to talk to ... she made you feel special. Yeah, because all it took was you'd walk in the gate, and [the facilitator] would stand there with a smile on her face, and that's all it took. And take your baby ... She's very enthusiastic about it all, too. She's so positive ... and it motivates us a little bit. (Focus group parents)

> Interpersonal skills, she [the facilitator] is non-threatening, calm, has beautiful communication skills and she's got terrific conflict resolution skills. Just her manner with people and she's never, ever threatening, even when it's a really difficult situation and we've had a few of those ... she's just got the best interpersonal skills, and that has to be number one ... She's got such a passion for children and wants to do whatever is best for the kids, and the parents. (School principal)

As these quotes illustrate, practitioners and parents shared views that facilitators needed to be good communicators who acted professionally and who demonstrated knowledge of children and the community service system.

Family-centred practice: focusing on parents and children

A distinguishing feature in my research groups was the family-centred approach used by facilitators. They worked in ways that combined early childhood development knowledge and family work practice, and this promoted positive outcomes for parents and their children. The facilitators were focused on providing high-quality early childhood learning environments that promoted natural conversations with parents about children and their development. Simultaneously, the facilitators also focused on parents, and their interactions with them ranged from hospitality to the mediation of relationship issues between participants:

> You're not just working with the children, you're not just working with the parents, you're working with the family. And the family's there because of their child. So I think it [child development knowledge] is pretty important. And often that's a friendly easy way in to talk to a parent about their child and their parenting, rather than their personal lives. (Facilitator)

As described earlier, another key factor in dual-focused groups is the ability of facilitators to effectively combine their interpersonal skills with child development, family work and service system knowledge. Facilitators' abilities to interact well with parents and children and to have knowledge that families can draw on, is highly important in this context:

> I think someone who's already got an understanding of child development because if you are going to be running it people are going to be discussing things and you don't want the discussion to [be ineffective] ... You would certainly be looking at some sort of interpersonal skills, conflict resolution, how to facilitate people getting on, you want to have some sort of negotiation skills ... You are dealing with such a huge amount of people, and complex families, service industry with red tape and you can't possibly do that job without having interpersonal skills. (School principal)

It is clear that facilitators who bring a combination of skills and knowledge to their work with parents and children enable dual-focused groups to provide an environment that is family centred. Facilitators should expect that they will be required to make decisions about the needs of the group or individual families and that their ability to engage parents in these decision-making processes will potentially lead to positive outcomes such as parental reassurance, successful referral to outside agencies, and better interpersonal relationships between participants.

The care factor: trust and engagement

The ability of facilitators to develop trust with participants is paramount to the support that parents will experience and to their ongoing engagement. Parents in my study gave numerous examples that illustrated the depth of the relationships that facilitators had developed with them. The need for facilitators to listen to parents and to demonstrate unconditional acceptance and respect for them is crucial. The ability to demonstrate these attitudes through genuine interest, care and help is vital to the well-being of parents and children:

> I think general acceptance of the parents is important. They [parents] experience a lot of stigma and judgment … so to know that they could come and be greeted by a friendly face who wasn't going to criticise them or judge them about the decisions that they'd made, or how they look, or what they're doing, I think was really important. And I guess I did get that feedback back from them about the importance of that, and just that they believed that I cared … (Facilitator)

Case study

With caring, trusting relationships in mind, facilitators also need to be reflective and to enable respectful, strengths-based relationships with parents to develop:

> I firmly believe people really can change just by being positively regarded by someone … in an environment where they feel affirmed … subtle things like making eye contact and sitting down with people and listening to them and just having a shift in your thinking – like this is a person who behaves in a particular way because of what has happened to them in the past … I suppose it's that thing about being alongside people rather than above them … You've got to like people, be kind to people, make allowances for people, understand where people are coming from and be quick on your feet about how you respond to a certain situation. Don't assume you know more than they do … respect people's way of doing things. (Facilitator)

This facilitator built trusting relationships with families and demonstrated genuine respect and acceptance of families' circumstances. Her ability to listen to parents and to engage in caring behaviours contributed significantly to these relationships, as did her ability to 'scaffold' new playgroup members' participation. This is an example of how parents' experiences of dual-focused groups can be linked to a facilitator's willingness to engage in respectful and self-reflective behaviours.

Creating a 'space'

The creation of a 'space' in which families experience the types of support described in Chapter 4 will only occur as a result of considerable reflection and planning by the facilitators. There are a number of elements that stand out as vital to the engagement of families and thus to the provision of multidimensional support in this type of early years setting.

Parents appreciate an environment that enables them to interact socially. This may consist of informal or formal opportunities such as the co-construction between parents and professionals of specific activities such as craft, cooking or sharing food. This type of enabling environment serves as an excellent platform for 'free encounters' (Geens and Vandenbroeck, 2013) within a social context that recognises and assists parents' agency within micro events. This leads to a process of confrontation, questioning, conversation and the co-construction of knowledge. It may also lead to parent-led conversations about the need for more formal types of support.

> Overwhelmingly, they [parents] say we just want to be here and talk to each other ... I think getting people just doing [things] together is really important ... You see people sitting around doing craft activities together ... that's where people talk about their lives ... it is a space for people to actually talk about what is important to them and what they do with their lives. Also for people to feel that someone is listening ... everybody has some sort of story, so I think providing places where people can do that is great. (Facilitator)

The nature of dual-focused groups and the 'free encounters' that happen within them means that there will sometimes be tension between what parents and facilitators expect in relation to parent–child interaction and this is something that needs to be negotiated. In my study a facilitator spoke of her struggle with this issue and about how she monitored the situation each week and sometimes decided that parents were in more need of support from each other, in which case she consciously interacted with children herself while parents interacted with one another:

> I guess for me I had to try and work [it] out ... if there was a child that we were having to spend a lot of time with because their parent was busy talking, we were probably making assumptions that was how that parent behaved at home, maybe that was wrong, we don't know whether at home that parent does a lot with that child and this was a break ... That is where it's difficult. Maybe this is that child's only opportunity to have someone sit down and play with and talk to them, you just don't know. (Facilitator)

Knowledge of the local service system: access to other information and resources

Having a thorough knowledge of local services for families and the referral pathways to more formal types of support is integral to the facilitation of dual-focused settings. The development of trusting relationships within an environment of 'free encounter' often means that the facilitator becomes a conduit for access to resources outside of the setting. Families in my study all spoke about this and said that they had accessed, or knew that they could access, assistance and help through this relationship:

> Yes, I can sort of go to anyone [facilitators] and say 'I'm having troubles can you help me' and they can sort of help you link into things like Department of Housing and you can go to any of the workers and talk to them and they can always be helpful with counselling and stuff if you're feeling a bit depressed … (Young parent)

> I don't know whether because she [the facilitator] has been doing this for so long or whatever but she's got the threads, the connections everywhere, and if she doesn't she will go and find them, build them, she's like a spider. (School principal)

Where possible it is also extremely useful for facilitators to respond to parent-identified concerns by coordinating other services or programmes which parents are able to access within the group environment.

> The parents actually sat right in the middle of where the kids were and talked … we had early childhood people from the health service come in over a number of weeks, we had the physiotherapist and the occupational therapist and the social worker, we have done quite a bit of that … (Facilitator)

The knowledge of local service systems and the ability to coordinate other forms of support for parents is a vital aspect of facilitation. It is crucial that there is relevant and timely access to information and resources from within these environments as these opportunities may not otherwise be available to families.

A closer look at facilitation

The engagement and ongoing participation of a broad range of families in dual-focused groups is dependent on the satisfaction and support that parents experience in the groups. This satisfaction and support is directly related to the critical role that facilitators play in creating accepting and responsive spaces for families. Insights have been provided above into various aspects of facilitation and these provide us with an understanding of the link between its effectiveness and the engagement and support of parents and children.

As we have seen, the types of support and resources that parents can potentially access in this type of service provision can affirm their roles as parents and enhance their interactions with their children. Given that the social and emotional development of young children is said to be influenced by the ways in which parent-support activities are delivered (Trivette and Dunst, 2008), the extent to which this happens in these types of early years settings is dependent upon the ways in which the groups are facilitated (Jackson, 2013).

In dual-focused early years settings children's developmental outcomes are potentially influenced by their interactions with other group participants and by the experience of their parents within the groups. In turn, parents' experiences in the groups are influenced by the relationships they develop with each other and with the facilitators. It is clear that the type of environments that promote these interdependent relationships, and which parents describe as supportive for themselves and their children, do not happen by accident. Promoting a social environment in which a diverse range of strengths, expectations and needs are recognised and catered for is a result of deliberate action by facilitators.

So far we have seen how facilitators are able to act in ways that demonstrate their belief that parents have existing capabilities and strengths, as well as the capacity for reflection and change. Focusing on encounters and diversity (Geens and Vandenbroeck, 2013) enabled parents to engage in these groups on an ongoing basis. The promotion of participatory experiences in which parents came together around a common interest and shared their collective knowledge enhanced their existing competencies and facilitated the acquisition of new knowledge (Berry and Letendre, 2004; Jackson, 2010).

🔑 Key idea: participatory experience

The concept of participatory experience is described by Dunst and Trivette (1996) and can be applied to the types of settings described in this book that are designed to bring parents together around the common interest of their children. An interest in their children's well-being combined with the need for adult social interaction, leads to the initial engagement of most families in these types of groups. By recognising the importance of both of these aspects to parental engagement, facilitators can build skilfully on parents' interests,

(Continues)

(Continued)

needs or concerns in ways that further engage them in co-constructed, social learning experiences.

Trivette and Dunst (2008) and others (see Geens and Vandenbroeck, 2013; Shonkoff and Phillips, 2000) offer further explanation as to why dual-focused settings have the potential to effectively engage a diverse range of families. These authors show that programmes that provide families with a combination of supported parent interaction and early childhood education experiences have greater than average effects on the development of both parents and their children. Participation by parents and children in the types of experiences facilitated for them in these settings contribute to what Dunst and Trivette (1996) have described as a 'feedback loop'. For example, positive outcomes such as social connectedness experienced early on in families' engagement in groups may lead to further participation and outcomes such as increased confidence in parenting and decreased social isolation.

As described earlier in this chapter the facilitator's function in my study fell into four categories: family-centred practice, the care factor, creating a 'space' and knowledge of the local service system. A closer look at what facilitators do can also be viewed in terms of the family-centred framework applied widely in early childhood intervention for children with special needs (Dunst and Trivette, 1996). The framework includes technical quality, relational practices and participatory practices that, when found in combination, provide the best outcomes for family well-being.

Technical qualities are the knowledge and skills that facilitators possess as a direct result of their training and experience. The main technical aspects in this context are expertise related to child development, the provision of early childhood learning experiences and family work. A facilitator's understanding of the local community and welfare service system and their professional knowledge of formal supports and referral pathways can also be considered part of the technical skills that they bring to the facilitation role.

Relational practices include facilitators' interpersonal skills, active listening skills and ability to be empathetic, caring and nurturing. These practices also include facilitators' ability to view parents as capable and to recognise their parenting capacities. Facilitators in dual-focused service provision need to utilise these traits and attributions to develop meaningful relationships with parents and to engage in processes of ongoing reflection that informs their behaviour and practice.

Participatory practices in this context include facilitators involving parents actively and meaningfully. They should seek and pay attention to parent input into the types of activities that are presented with particular emphasis on providing a range of supports within mainstream, social environments based on what parents say they want. Similarly, facilitators will at times need to engage in processes that address particular issues and promote positive relational growth among parents.

Recommended further reading

Dunst, C. and Trivette, C. (1996) 'Empowerment, effective helpgiving practices and family-centered care', *Paediatric Nursing*, 22(4): 334–37.

The framework described above allows for compartmentalisation of the work that facilitators do in dual-focused groups in order to fully examine their roles. However, the real strength of this work lies in the ability to combine the three components described above to provide a holistic, family-centred approach to working with families. The ways in which facilitators situate their professional expertise and beliefs in parents' capabilities within caring and respectful relationships enables, truly supportive environments to be created.

Above all, when facilitators combine relational and participatory practices rather than relying on technical knowledge alone, parents potentially experience psychological benefits from their participation (Dawson and Berry, 2002; Dunst and Trivette, 1996). When groups are facilitated in this way parents are more likely to experience emotional support, decreased isolation and increased confidence in parenting, which are known to influence children's positive developmental outcomes and to assist in the reduction of abusive or neglectful behaviours by parents (Bowes, 2000; Dunst and Trivette, 1996; Higgins and Katz, 2008).

Further, it has been found that the most immediate influences on parenting behaviour include: knowledge of child development; attitudes and beliefs about children; and parents' ability to view events from children's points of view and to make positive interpretations of their behaviour (Centre for Community Child Health, 2007). Facilitators play a crucial role in creating environments that assist parents to enhance and construct such skills and knowledge, guided through the substantial relationships they build with them.

It is useful now to point out that dual-focused service provision usually occurs at a time when parents are most likely to be interested in finding social interaction opportunities for their young children. It follows then that facilitators need an understanding of the window of opportunity that these contexts provide to engage families and build trusting relationships early in children's lives. By consistently providing opportunities for parents to experience authentic, mutually rewarding interactions with their children and with other adults, and positively exposing them to family-strengthening resources, they will be creating environments that are characteristic of effectively facilitated programmes as described in the literature (Ghate and Hazel, 2002; Shonkoff and Phillips, 2000; Trivette and Dunst, 2008).

This being said, as discussed in Chapter 4, adopting a family-centred approach in this context also requires facilitators to take action to address relationship or other group issues that sometimes arise. In my study, facilitators were aware of these types of circumstances and showed skill in attending to them in a timely and appropriate manner, which resulted in positive relationship outcomes for participants.

Their reflection on the tension between a parent focus and a child focus in the groups also demonstrated that they understood that their groups needed to provide for both children and parents. This understanding is supported in the literature which suggests that programmes need to maintain a balanced focus on parents and children and that programmes that provide for parents and children together lead to longer-term developmental outcomes, particularly for children from disadvantaged circumstances (see Jackson, 2010).

The dilemma described above is caused by two factors:

- an understanding of the social context of parenting and the connection between parental experience of supportive interpersonal relationships and positive outcomes for children; and
- an understanding of the importance of positive adult–child interactions to children's development.

These factors suggest that facilitators need to know their parents well and attempt to cater to their needs appropriately. The development of deep relationships between facilitators and parents leads to real understandings of families' needs and responses that are contextual. This means that sometimes facilitators will enable parents to spend a lot of time together and interact more with the children themselves. At other times they will encourage more interaction between parents and children. In this way both sets of needs will be met and the environment will be responsive to children and their parents (Jackson, 2010).

The successful engagement of families in dual-focused, early years settings is complex. It requires facilitators to:

- accept families the way they are, regardless of circumstance and invite their input into the programme;
- use family-friendly strategies that reduce practical and psychological barriers to access;
- combine technical knowledge with relational and participatory practices to provide a family-centred environment that is non-judgemental and responsive;
- facilitate flexible access to informal and formal support systems for families;
- have in-depth knowledge of local services systems and utilise a multidisciplinary approach; and

- engage in ongoing professional development and supervision that informs their practice.

The critical link between the role of a facilitator and effectiveness in this context is summed up succinctly in the following quote from one of my study participants: 'She [the facilitator] is outstanding and so it makes an outstanding playgroup. If you had a good facilitator it would make a good playgroup, there is a direct correlation' (School principal).

Reflective activities: creating a nurturing community

This chapter has discussed the critical role of facilitation in dual-focused groups. It has demonstrated how the engagement and ongoing participation of diverse families in this type of service provision reflects the satisfaction and support that they experience. Importantly, it has highlighted that this satisfaction and support is directly related to the role that facilitators play in creating accepting and responsive environments for families.

1. You have been asked to facilitate a group for parents and young children. What are the key elements you would consider to ensure the group engages families and encourages their ongoing participation?
2. 'Free encounters' are an important aspect of social interaction. Describe a positive and a negative example and explain the consequences of each.
3. Explain your understanding of participatory practice and describe how it is linked to technical qualities and relational practices.

References

Berry, M. and Letendre, J. (2004) 'Lambs and lions: the role of psychoeducational groups in enhancing relationship skills and social networks', *Groupwork*, 14(1): 30–45.

Bowes, J. (2000) 'Parents' response to parent education and support programs', *National Child Protection Clearing House Newsletter*, 8(2): 12–21.

Centre for Community Child Health (2007) 'Effective community-based services', Policy Brief no. 6, accessed 2 December 2007 at www.rch.org.au/ccch/policybriefs.cfm.

Dawson, K. and Berry, M. (2002) 'Engaging families in child welfare services: an evidenced-based approach to best practice', *Child Welfare*, 81(2): 293–317.

Dunst, C. and Trivette, C. (1996) 'Empowerment, effective helpgiving practices and family-centered care', *Paediatric Nursing*, 22(4): 334–37.

Geens, N. and Vandenbroeck, M. (2013) 'Early childhood education and care as a space for social support in urban contexts of diversity', *European Early Childhood Education Research Journal*, 21(3): 407–9.

Ghate, D. and Hazel, N. (2002) *Parenting in Poor Environments. Stress, Support and Coping*. London: Policy Research Bureau.

Higgins, D. and Katz, I. (2008) 'Enhancing service systems for protecting children', *Family Matters*, (80): 43–51.

Jackson, D. (2010) 'A place to "be": supported playgroups, a model of relational, social support for parents and children', University of Western Sydney, Sydney.

Jackson, D. (2013) 'Creating a place to "be": unpacking the facilitation role in three supported playgroups in Australia', *European Early Childhood Education Research Journal*, 21(1): 77–93.

Shonkoff, J. and Phillips, D. (2000) *From Neurons to Neighborhoods*. Washington, DC: National Academy Press.

Trivette, C. and Dunst, C. (2008) 'Community-based parent support programs', *Encyclopaedia on Early Childhood Development*, accessed 1 October 2009 at: www.enfant-encyclopedie.com/pages/PDF/Trivette-DunstANGxp.pdf.

CHAPTER 6

Nurturing parents, nurturing children

Chapter overview

This chapter will provide an insight into the developmental benefits of informal, social spaces for parents and children. It will highlight the importance of understanding the 'secure base' behaviours of young children and the 'letting go' behaviours of parents and will demonstrate why it is necessary to encourage responsiveness to children rather than overemphasising parent involvement in their play. Again by drawing on research into the Australian supported playgroup model (Jackson, 2010) a greater understanding of these, and other concepts such as repertoires of practice (Rogoff et al., 2007), will be developed. This will foster the implementation of practice that is family centred rather than child or parent centred, which enables the holistic provision of services that encompass the strengths and needs of all participants. The chapter concludes with a reiteration of how dual-focused groups can be environments that play a significant role in the landscape of early childhood education, particularly for 0–3-year-old children, in regard to the fostering of secure attachment and enhancement of young children's developmental outcomes.

Introduction

Nurturing children's development lies at the heart of dual-focused groups. Groups such as supported playgroups provide important early childhood learning settings that enhance children's social interaction and foster positive interactions with their parents, peers and other adults. Significantly, groups such as these have the potential to provide socially supportive spaces for parents and safe, stimulating environments where children can play in close proximity to them. This enables children to explore and participate independently and to return to the 'secure base' of their parents, the combination of which is known to contribute to the reduction of separation anxiety and to the development of secure infant–parent attachment relationships (Appleyard and Berlin, 2007; Bowlby, 1988; Reebye et al., 2009).

Children aged 0–3 years are often highly represented in dual-focused groups and sometimes this is the only early childhood setting they attend. Therefore it is important that children are engaged in play environments that are characterised by the provision of quality learning activities across all developmental domains with many opportunities for solitary, parallel and associative play interactions.

In this type of service provision it is also common for parents of very young children to sit together and talk while their children sit on their laps or play on the floor at their feet. The interactions between parents and children in this age range are also characterised by young children exploring the playgroup environment and returning frequently to their parents. Parents are generally responsive to their children each time they return and often leave their conversations to attend to their children's needs or participate in activities at their children's requests. It is important to note too that there are fewer interactions of this nature between the 3–5-year-old children in these types of groups as these children tend to play independently with their peers and are more inclined to seek their parent's attention periodically. They also often engage in interactions with practitioners and with parents other than their own, which encourages their social development.

It is therefore important that facilitators understand the importance of creating environments that enhance attachment between parents and children and reduce separation anxiety. The play environment should be designed so children and parents can maintain visual contact with each other and come and go from each other freely. If special activities are organised for parents during group sessions, it helps if children are free to move to and from their parents at will. This strategy, while more difficult to manage in terms of noise and interruption, enables children to return to their parents as necessary and assists parents to participate more fully in activities or discussions without worrying about their children's well-being. Groups such as these provide a safe place for both parents and children to develop secure attachment behaviours in the presence of one another and with the support of the groups' facilitators.

Case study

Well, we've got one family I know in particular, who had never been involved in any sort of schooling or pre-schooling. A mother with one child, difficult home situation, and moved several times to escape a difficult home situation so very, very close bond with this child and vice versa … [there were] very few social skills on the child's part and very, very clingy, and the mother [was] very unwilling to let the child do anything, possibly because of what they'd experienced prior to that. Coming here and being involved in the playgroup certainly has allowed the strings to be lessened, if you like. This child is now at school … I've seen a huge progression last year in the playgroup … they came in and were very welcomed and the child was allowed to develop very slowly, one friend at a time or sitting in the corner for a little while and then gradually coming in and sharing toys so that manifested reasonably slowly … the difference with pre-school and the playgroup is that the mother didn't have to leave the child and go through that immediate separation and huge anxiety that she was feeling … She [the mother] felt very secure in the playgroup so the child then felt very secure, because whatever mum feels the child feels … (School principal)

I just hoped that N would actually be able to leave my side. Because when we first started going to playgroup I'd spend two hours and he'd just be still at my side, or he'd say, Mummy, come with, come – and I found I couldn't socialise because I was always having to do all activities with him while the other mums had their cups of tea. So I just used to long for him to be able to leave me and go and play and have some fun with other children. It's taken a long time, but I think he's there. (Parent)

Young children's development in dual-focused groups

Young children's development is positively influenced in environments where their relationships with parents or carers are nurtured and where they are able to engage in quality play experiences: both child driven and adult directed (Bodrova and Leong, 2003; Elliott, 2006; Ginsburg, 2007). Dual-focused groups such as the supported playgroups are likely to play a role in the stimulation and establishment of neural and biological pathways that lay the foundation for children's emotional, social and intellectual development (Jackson, 2010).

The social interaction and play aspects of these types of groups are significant because, by their nature, they provide opportunities for children to engage in child-driven play experiences and adult-directed learning activities. There is also clear evidence that groups such as these potentially provide access to learning experiences that parents may not provide for children at home and facilitators have an important role in modelling simple play activities. There is also a clear emphasis on child interaction and the development of social relationships both with their peers and with adults. All of these are characteristics that contribute to what are described in the literature as effective Western early childhood learning environments (Fleer et al., 2009; Rushton and Larkin, 2001).

This being said, further attention needs to be drawn to an issue that arose among parents in my study who referred to their perceived laziness or apathy at providing activities for their children at home, particularly those activities perceived as 'messy'. This could be interpreted as parents experiencing guilt because of Western, middle-class expectations of what they 'should' be providing for their children. Dual-focused groups provide opportunities to demonstrate that there are many ways in which parents can interact with their children. But it is important to highlight the potential within these groups for parents to experience feelings of inferiority if they are not comfortable providing certain types of play experiences. Awareness of this issue is an important aspect of providing a space for families where parents can 'be', and practitioners, while providing interesting educational environments for children, need to be mindful that their practices truly respect the diversity of participants. Practitioners need to ask parents what they think is important for their young children and why, and provide quality learning environments that do not inadvertently reflect a 'one size fits all' approach to children's play.

A closer examination of children's engagement in play within dual-focused groups demonstrates how important this type of service provision can be to their development. Ginsburg (2007) is a strong advocate for community-based programmes that bring to light the critical nature of children's play. He argues that parents, through observing their children playing or by interacting in child-driven play are given a unique opportunity to view the world through their children's eyes. This, he suggests, enables parents to understand their children more fully and to communicate with them more effectively. Supported playgroups, and other similar models, provide these opportunities and parents appreciate sociable settings in which they can observe their children's interactions with their peers and other adults and where they can become involved in activities with their children. For some parents these types of services may be the only opportunities their children have to play and interact in this way.

Further, this type of early childhood setting provides many opportunities for children to engage in child-driven play in which parents are passive observers rather than participants. As discussed in the preceding chapter, the perceived lack of involvement by parents in children's play sometimes causes a dilemma for some parents and group facilitators who become concerned that the focus should be on the encouragement of parent–child interactions in play. While parent interaction in children's play is highly valuable in its own right, Ginsburg (2007) and others (Kagan et al., 2009; Zigler and Bishop-Josef, 2009) assert that child-driven play, in which parents are either not present or are passive observers, helps children develop characteristics that are intrinsic to resilience. This was demonstrated in my study when children gradually became less anxious and more independently involved in playgroup activities while their parents were in close proximity but not involved with them directly. It is of course understood that in some cases parents' lack of interaction with their children in these environments is, for other reasons, a justifiable concern for practitioners. Nevertheless, a better understanding of the link between child-driven, independent play and the development of resilience assists in developing new perspectives related to this aspect of dual-focused groups.

The creation of social spaces in which children play in close proximity to their parents also provides opportunities for children to observe their parents' engagement in nurturing, adult friendships. The work of several authors (Rogoff et al., 2003, 2007; Swick, 2001) elucidates the developmental gains that are achieved when young children participate in everyday cultural practices and activities alongside their parents. Young children monitor events around them and learn through observation (Garbarino and Abramowitz, 1992; Rogoff et al., 2003) and in many cases they are able to learn complex concepts such as language rules or categorisation schemes through modelled examples, without further explanation or adult mediation (Rogoff et al., 2003).

🔑 Key idea: repertoires of practice

Bourdieu (1977) suggests that experience of one's environment and routine occurrences leads to the development of subconscious tendencies to behaviours. Unspoken understandings that children acquire through participation in everyday events are a key part of how they organise their interactions and how these understandings become 'submerged in consciousness' (Rogoff et al., 2007). This type of peripheral, observant learning contributes to what Rogoff et al. (2007) describe as 'repertoires of practice', that is, the variety of practices that individuals become familiar with and are able to apply under different circumstances.

It could be argued that participation in dual-focused groups may assist the development of children's repertoires of practice in many areas. The

(Continues)

(Continued)

following quote draws our particular attention to the possibility that children's friendship behaviours may be influenced by their third-party observation of their parents' social interaction patterns at playgroups:

> I realised that you don't actually need that much stuff [equipment], it's what goes on between people [that] is the important thing I think, often for those children. It's interesting, it just struck me and I remember with my own kids, I wanted them to grow up with a strong sense of how important it was to have friends and what that meant and I guess for [the playgroup] kids, even though some of their mothers do just sit and talk, that's probably not actually a bad thing for those kids to be seeing people [parents] having those sorts of conversations and [to] play in that context. (Facilitator)

Children's repertoires of practice also include those related to attachment and exploratory behaviours as described by Bowlby (1988). Attachment repertoires include the behaviours of approaching, following, hugging, cuddling and clinging which bring children close to their parents. Exploratory repertoires take children away from their parents to walk, climb, run and investigate the world. As children experiment with these two types of behaviours, parents must be aware of the need to demonstrate two complementary types of behaviours: protective behaviours that provide young children with safety, care and nurture, and 'letting go' behaviours that encourage and enable children to explore and participate in the environment without fear. By engaging in these behaviours parents provide 'secure bases' for children that enable them to balance independence with care and protection thus assisting in the development of secure attachment behaviours (Appleyard and Berlin, 2007; Jordan and Sketchley, 2009; Reebye et al., 2009).

Dual-focused groups can provide optimal environments for young children that enable them to explore and develop independence alongside their parents. Groups such as these have the potential to contribute positively to secure attachment and reduce separation anxiety for many children and their parents because they enhance parental opportunities to engage in the complementary behaviours described above.

As noted earlier, many children attending this type of early childhood setting are likely to be 3 years of age or under and as such are likely to be seeking opportunities to explore. Therefore, the ability for children to leave their parents, engage independently and then return to the security of their parents is an important and sometimes underestimated aspect of service provision. It is not unusual for practitioners and parents to have limited understandings about the influences of this type of service provision on children's secure attachment behaviours. There can be tension because of the apparent competing foci of dual-focused groups: are the groups for parents, children, or both? However, concerns related to parents socialising with one another, rather than engaging constantly with their children in play activities, are possibly misplaced in terms of children's development. By using attachment theory as a lens through which to view this issue it becomes apparent that the opportunities that these groups provide for young children's safe, independent exploration is likely to assist their feelings of competence and control over their environments, and to influence secure attachment to their parents (Appleyard and Berlin, 2007; Reebye et al., 2009).

This chapter provides us with insights into the developmental benefits that groups such as supported playgroups can provide for young children. It also highlights the need for practitioners working in dual-focused groups to understand the 'secure base' behaviours of young children in order to encourage responsive parenting styles that encompass protective and 'letting go' behaviours. Clearer understanding of these concepts enables a natural shift in practitioners' attention to encouraging and modelling adult responsiveness to children, rather than overemphasising parent involvement in their play.

Such an understanding helps to promote practice that is neither child nor parent centred but family centred, enabling the provision of services that encompass the strengths and needs of all participants. It also assists in the appreciation of the ecological nature of service provision and the need for reflective valuing of the social and pedagogical aspects of early childhood services such as supported playgroups (Jackson, 2010; Vandenbroeck et al., 2009).

Dual-focused groups also have the potential to play a significant role in children's transitions to new settings such as formal childcare or school. Children's responsiveness and attachment to adults other than their parents is fostered in these type of groups and attachment theory again provides us with a framework to explain the importance of environments such as these in children's transitions.

Research undertaken in Western cultures such as Australia suggests that infants form hierarchies of attachment, with mothers generally being the primary attachment figure (Sims and Hutchins, 1999). Once secure attachment is formed with the primary figure, children are more likely to respond positively to other adults and go on to develop further attachment relationships with significant others, such as caregivers. Moreover, children's interactional patterns with their parents shape their expectations of how others will respond. Ideally, through secure attachment relationships with their primary carers, children develop 'working models' for other responsive and accessible relationships (Jackson, 2010).

Cross-cultural research also suggests that in communities where exclusive mother care is not practised, children form strong and secure primary attachments to more than one person (Sims and Hutchins, 1999). While it is not suggested here that dual-focused groups parallel situations where primary care is shared, linking cross-cultural evidence like this demonstrates the potential for groups such as these to be places where children can develop substantial relationships with significant others.

It is known that parent–child attachment influences children's social and emotional development and that those children who are less securely attached to their primary caregivers are likely to experience difficulties adjusting to pre-school and school (Smart et al., 2008). Groups such as supported playgroups enable young children to explore new environments and relationships with other adults because the environments promote secure attachment relationships with their parents. Parents and children transitioning from home to playgroup together enables parents to scaffold their children in situations which they may have found difficult to negotiate alone. That is, dual-focused groups create a 'zone of proximal development' (Vygotsky, 1978) in which parents and facilitators guide children's developing, independent behaviour.

Transitioning together in environments which parents find supportive also helps to reduce parental anxiety and optimises the potential for the development of caring, friendly relationships between parents and facilitators. In these ways, children are able to observe their parents' interactions with these other adults and are likely to infer that these people are safe people to interact with themselves. Through the process known as social referencing (Sims and Hutchins, 1999), dual-focused groups are able to create environments in which children can positively reference their own behaviour to that of their parents and build trusting relationships over time with adults other than their parents, such as practitioners and other parents. Again, this type of service provides a place in which parents and their children are able to engage in multifaceted, co-constructed learning that enhances their development.

This chapter has described aspects of the early childhood learning environments that are able to be created in dual-focused groups. The discussion would be incomplete, however, without reference to the preceding chapters that demonstrate the ways in which groups such as these need to be effectively facilitated to support the well-being of parents. An ecological perspective shows the interconnectedness of the early learning space, the role of the professional and parent support, and how these function together to enhance children's developmental outcomes.

Creating well-facilitated, supportive, social spaces that nurture parents' well-being and reduce their social isolation is critical to the provision of quality early childhood environments for children. Groups such as supported playgroups can play a significant role in the landscape of early childhood education, particularly for 0–3-year-old children. The potential for dual-focused service provision such as this to foster secure attachment and enhance the developmental outcomes of young children should not be underestimated.

Reflective activities: children's development in dual-focused models

This chapter discussed the developmental benefits of dual-focused groups that provide informal, social spaces for parents and children. It highlighted how important it is for practitioners to understand the 'secure base' behaviours of young children and the 'letting go' behaviours of parents in order to foster young children's secure attachment. The concept of repertoires of practice was also discussed in relation to family centred, rather than child- or parent-centred practice demonstrating how dual-focused groups can play a significant role in the landscape of early childhood education, particularly for 0–3-year-old children.

1. Imagine that you are the facilitator of a dual-focused group for parents and young children. Describe the way you would set up the play environment to encourage secure attachment in young children.
2. You are the facilitator for a group of 0–5-year-olds and their parents. A parent is upset because he thinks that there are too many parents talking and not interacting in activities with their children. What would be your response to this parent and why?
3. Sometimes parents involved in supported playgroups or similar types of groups feel guilty because they do not engage in some of the play activities that practitioners organise for their children. What would you do to address this situation?

References

Appleyard, K. and Berlin, L. (2007) 'Supporting healthy relationships between young children and their parents: lessons from attachment theory and research', accessed 17 October 2009 at: http://sanford.duke.edu/centers/child/eca/Attachment/index.htm.

Bodrova, E. and Leong, D. (2003) 'The importance of being playful', *Educational Leadership*, 60(7): 50–3.

Bourdieu, P. (1977) *Outline of a Theory of Practice*. trans. R. Nice. Cambridge: Cambridge University Press.

Bowlby, J. (1988) *A Secure Base*. New York: Basic Books.

Elliott, A. (2006) 'Early childhood education: pathways to quality and equity for all children', Australian Education Review 50, Australian Council for Educational Research, Melbourne.

Fleer, M., Tonyan, H., Mantilla, A. and Rivalland, C. (2009) 'Play and learning in Australia', in I. Pramling-Samuelsson and M. Fleer (eds), *Play and Learning in Early Childhood Settings. International Perspectives*. Dordrecht: Springer. pp. 51–80.

Garbarino, J. and Abramowitz, R. (1992) 'The ecology of human development', in J. Garbarino (ed.), *Children and Families in the Social Environment*. 2nd edn. New York: Walter de Gruyter. pp. 11–33.

Ginsburg, K. (2007) 'The importance of play in promoting healthy child development and maintaining strong parent–child bonds', *Paediatrics*, 119(1): 182–91.

Jackson, D. (2010) 'A place to "be": supported playgroups, a model of relational, social support for parents and children', University of Western Sydney, Sydney.

Jordan, B. and Sketchley, R. (2009) 'A stitch in time saves nine: preventing and responding to the abuse and neglect of infants', *Child Abuse Prevention Issues*, 30, accessed 2 August 2009 at: http://www.aifs.gov.au/ nch/pubs/issues/issues30/issues30.html

Kagan, S.L., Scott-Little, C. and Stebbins Frelow, V. (2009) 'Linking play to early learning and development guidelines', *Zero to Three*, 30(1): 19–25.

Reebye, P.N., Ross, S.E. and Jamieson, M.A. (2009) 'A literature review of child–parent/caregiver attachment theory and cross-cultural practices influencing attachment', accessed 1 September 2009 at: www. attachmentacrosscultures.org/research/

Rogoff, B., Moore, L., Najafi, B., Dexter, A., Correa-Chavez, M. and Solis, J. (2007) 'Children's development of cultural repertoires through participation in everyday routines and practices', in J.E. Grusec and P.D. Hastings (eds), *Handbook of Socialisation: Theory and Research*. New York: The Guildford Press. pp. 490–515.

Rogoff, B., Paradise, R., Mejia Arauz, R., Correa-Chavez, M. and Angelillo, C. (2003) 'Firsthand learning through intent participation', *Annual Review of Psychology*, 54: 175–203.

Rushton, S. and Larkin, E. (2001) 'Shaping the learning environment: connecting developmentally appropriate practices to brain research', *Early Childhood Education Journal*, 29(1): 25–33.

Sims, M. and Hutchins, T. (1999) 'Positive transitions', *Australian Journal of Early Childhood*, 24(3): 12–16.

Smart, D., Sanson, A., Baxter, J., Edwards, B. and Hayes, A. (2008) *Home-to-School Transitions for Financially Disadvantaged Children*. Final report. Sydney: The Smith Family.

Swick, K. (2001) 'Nurturing decency through caring and serving during the early childhood years', *Early Childhood Education Journal*, 29(2): 121–25.

Vandenbroeck, M., Roets, G. and Snoeck, A. (2009) 'Immigrant mothers crossing borders: nomadic identities and multiple belongings in early childhood education', *European Early Childhood Education Research Journal*, 17(2): 203–16.

Vygotsky, L.S. (1978) *Mind in Society: The Development of Higher Psychological Processes*. Cambridge, MA: Harvard University Press.

Zigler, E. and Bishop-Josef (2009) 'Play under siege', *Zero to Three*, 30(1): 5–11.

LEARNING TO LEARN IN SUPPORTED PLAYGROUPS

CHAPTER 7

Children learning in collaboration with adults

Chapter overview

We have argued in the first part of this book that it is in the act of doing things that early learning occurs and that this learning is deep and personal. The way that we are treated by others interacts with and shapes our immediate response and may shape longer-term dispositions towards our participation in interactions with others. Part 2 has shown how supported playgroups offer a space for all the participants to be with others and extend their repertoires of practice through sociable activity. This first chapter of Part 3 reviews and exemplifies some of the most influential ideas on supporting children's learning through interaction.

In essence the recommendations from research examining both parents' and practitioners' interactions with children learning are simple: engage in genuine, respectful and interested dialogue with the child. Such interactions are usually everyday features of children's lives and dual-focus groups enable parents, children and practitioners to extend their vocabulary of interaction through sharing space with others. Potentially all the participants in the group can learn more about how sound, movement and gesture in everyday interactions work together to form a sophisticated conversation with a baby or toddler. This chapter reflects on the importance of some of the different elements of conversation which researchers suggest are influential in shaping children's skills in learning, such as allowing space for the child to be able to steer the activity, allowing for turn-taking in the dance of control between the participants, trying to seek joint insights, drawing attention to thinking, and connecting ideas over time. It is suggested that practitioners may find these elements helpful in reviewing their own interactions and in affirming the skills of families.

Research into effective interaction in early education settings

We have already established in Chapter 3 that one of the key focuses for practitioners facilitating dual-focus groups is to enhance children's potential for learning by supporting the parent–child dyad. Part 3 of this book reports on research carried out to investigate the nature of interactions in support of children's activities in Stay and Play sessions in several children's centres in England. There are many reviews of the research evidence supporting the advantages for children where practitioners and parents adopt a constructivist approach to supporting learning, that is, an approach that facilitates some opportunities for children to be involved in developing and applying knowledge for themselves (Athey, 2007; MacNaughton, 2003; Schweinhart et al., 2005). This chapter summarises the arguments informing the promotion of particular types of interaction that potentially benefit children's engagement with future learning.

The most cited and influential study of the impact of different types of preschool experience is the Ypsilanti Preschool Curriculum Demonstration Project from the USA, usually called the Highscope study. It has frequently been used to argue that children who experience a play-based curriculum with a balance of adult-led and child-initiated activity develop a more independent self-managing outlook over the life course (Weikart et al., 1978).

The study is persuasive because it investigated a sample of children from a disadvantaged area who were randomly assigned to three different pre-school experiences and one that had no pre-school experience. The parents of the 22 children in the Highscope group were also encouraged to support the programme through a weekly home visit lasting 1.5 hours. Twenty three children were allocated to a pre-school offering formal 'classroom'-oriented activities and 23 children were allocated to a setting that offered more of a free-play environment. The progress of this group was compared with 55 children who received no pre-school programme, and the findings showed increased Intelligence Quotient (IQ) scores for all those in the pre-school groups. The IQ gains for all three groups were lost over time, however, the socialisation outcomes for the Highscope group were seen to have a significant effect at age 15, 27 and 35 (Schweinhart et al., 2005). The Highscope programme claims to focus particular attention on 'active learning' and 'independence' by encouraging children to reflect verbally on experience, feelings and activities, including an emphasis on planning and reviewing activity.

Larger-scale studies in New Zealand (Wylie and Thompson, 2003) and the UK (Sylva et al., 2010) suggest similar medium-term findings: that more positive social and intellectual benefits accrue for children in programmes that adopt the type of pedagogy outlined above. That is, one that affirms children as active learners and provides opportunities for them to lead some of their own activities and to engage with supportive adults. These studies have identified several interactive strategies as features of outstanding and effective practice in collaborative learning: scaffolding, co-construction and sustained shared thinking (SST) (Sylva et al., 2010: 4; Wylie and Thompson, 2003).

This chapter explores these recommendations for interaction styles in some depth to identify their value as strategies when working with parents. These models have often been developed to describe interactions with children aged 4 and 5 years, careful consideration has to be given to whether they are appropriate to the tasks offered in parent and child groups, meaningful to parents or practitioners and relevant to younger children.

Much of the early education literature used to advise practitioners is not directly located in dual-focus groups. Scaffolding literature is often set in research or classroom contexts, while research on guided participation is set in home contexts. However, both speculate about the potential for cultural patterns of interaction to impact on children's thinking and their ability to reflect on thinking (often referred to as metacognition).

> Such differences may lead to variation in children's skill in managing their own attention and observation, and in managing verbal interactions with adults as conversational peers.
>
> I am not advocating that children should experience only these forms of interaction or be hot-housed in them but rather that children with more exposure to these types of interaction have been shown to do well in primary education. 'These skills and interactional practices are differently useful for participation in varying institutional contexts such as formal schooling and economic activities'. (Rogoff et al., 1998: 245)

Encouraging the child to take control

In the 1970s, Wood et al. researched parents' tutoring in problem-solving tasks under research conditions. They identified the term 'scaffolding' and went on to elaborate what they perceived to be more effective ways of helping children to solve puzzles (Wood et al, 1976). The term 'scaffolding' relates to helping the child to solve problems by drawing attention to, and reflecting on, significant aspects of the problem rather than presenting them with a solution.

Bruner (1986) sets out a model of effective tutoring for 3- and 5-year-olds where the adult becomes the 'consciousness for two'. The adult controls the focus of attention by demonstrating the direction of the outcome of the task, breaking it down into achievable segments matched to the child's understanding and managing the situation so the child can recognise achievements and repeat them. The adult then gradually hands over control of individual elements as the child gains mastery over them.

The process of scaffolding is argued to have advantages over the direct transmission of knowledge because it places responsibility for learning with the individual learner rather than the 'teacher'. It offers a greater sense of ownership of knowledge and suggests to the learner that the creation of knowledge is an ongoing, active process to participate in, rather than one in which the answer is presented by others (Hohmann and Weikart, 2002). Compared with notions of shaping behaviours, a key feature of scaffolding involves the tutor simplifying the learner's role in the task rather than simplifying the overall goal of the task (Greenfield, 1984).

Allowing the child to take control of the activity in order to gain a sense of responsibility for managing it involves two things: the adult drawing attention to the significant features of managing the activity, and helping the child to work out how to control those features. The adult encourages the child to reflect on what is taking place and how he or she is managing that change but the idea of an end point or outcome is in the adult's mind and the child is being guided towards that end point with scope for trial and error. This is a process for thinking about actions, cause and effect, and of using language to help manage thinking and learning.

In the example which follows Jane, aged 3 years, has been encouraged to come to a table set up to make mini pizzas in a Stay and Play group with her mother Mary. Pam is a practitioner from the local children's centre that supports the parent and child group which meets in a church hall. She has set up the activity, the dough bases are already made, there is a tomato sauce topping already prepared and various toppings to choose from. Pam is supporting some parents with their children and children on their own who have younger siblings.

Example 1

Mary, Jane's mother, sits on a chair at her shoulder and she talks Jane through the process of preparing the pizza; first asking her if she knows what all the ingredients are identifying mushroom, pepper, cheese, tomato. Mary identifies each correctly. Mary asks 'so what do we put on top of the pizza?'

'What we do is … this is what we do' says Jane who has seen Pam cutting the vegetables. She takes a knife and tries to cut the pepper.

'I don't think you'll do it Jane,' suggests mum who proceeds to help hold the knife and pepper, physically helping her to cut the pepper.

'Get the flowers,' says Jane. 'The flower, where's the flower?' Mary points to the seeds, 'those are the seeds'.

'Seeds?' asks Jane.

'Do they look like flowers? Do you want to make the pizza now?'

'Yes.' Then Mary asks Jane if she knows what this is, showing her the saucers of tomato puree 'erm …'

'It's called tomato puree.'

'Tomato puree' Jane repeats, 'so you've got to put this on there.' Jane says that she wants to do this by herself and mum confirms this is ok and quickly says that Jane has put enough on.

'What do you think you should do now?' asks Mary.

'Spread it all over the place' says Jane. Mary encourages her to do this and Jane carefully spreads the puree over the triangle of pre-prepared base. A little puree overspills the base.

'Oh its come off' says Jane.

'It's all right, put it on' says Mary calmly.

Jane continues to spread for a while and then Mary asks what she would like to put on it and Jane says that she wants to put on tomato and cheese. Mary then encourages her to get some tomato asking how many she thinks she needs. Jane counts out pieces of tomato 'one … two … three'.

Mary says that this is enough and asks what they are going to do with them.

'Put that on there' says Jane. 'Ok. That's right. Now what?' and Jane says that she wants to put cheese on again. Mary confirms this and asks if she wants to use a spoon which Jane proceeds to do, sprinkling cheese carefully over the pizza using a large metal spoon until Mary says that she thinks that is enough.

'I've made it' says Jane. Mary confirms in a well done tone that she has done it and asks what she is going to do with it now.

'Put it in there' says Jane. Mary asks what that is called and Jane says foil and proceeds to pull out a long length of foil. Mary helps her to cut and explains that they will wrap it up to take home. Jane then proceeds to make a second piece by herself putting on pepper and mushrooms in addition to cheese and tomato. She then takes a spoon of cheese and starts to eat the grated cheese from the large spoon taking three spoons of the cheese.

There are clear expectations of all those involved in the activity about how the pizza-making will turn out, Mary asks closed questions to check vocabulary and clarifies the name for the seeds. Mary regulates Jane's activity while at the same time encouraging her to do as much as possible and at the end of the activity, Jane's comments such 'OK. That's right. Now what?' echo the sorts of phrases that Mary uses to monitor the progress and next steps of the activity. Thus language used by the adult becomes a scaffold for the thinking of the child and helps the adult to gain an insight into where the child might need further guidance or not. Over the course of the activity there is a move towards control being given to the child and is completed by Jane producing a second pizza with no further direction.

Promoting child-led interaction

Jordan (2004) points out that a variety of interpretations have developed in relation to the term scaffolding. She states that some people interpret scaffolding as being the support given to children to get them into the zone in which learning occurs and this may involve children engaging in provocative activities with minimal adult interaction. Jordan reasserts the need to apply pedagogical terms thoughtfully in order to retain their integrity. She affirms the value of the term 'scaffolding' as described by Wood (1998) as being linked to active adult support rather than passive monitoring.

Jordan goes on to show how in her own research of practitioners supporting pre-school learning she perceived the need to emphasise the idea of co-construction as distinct from scaffolding. Her argument is that interactions which support learning can be more tightly or less tightly controlled by the adult's goal and she retains the term 'scaffolding' for interactions with a tighter control towards the adult's objectives (as in the pizza example above). Jordan uses the term 'co-construction' for interactions where there is a more open and exploratory exchange between the adult and child. She states that co-construction places emphasis on teachers and children studying meanings and understandings together in favour of acquiring facts. 'Studying meaning requires teachers and children to make sense of the world, interpreting and understanding activities and observations as they interact with each other' (Jordan, 2004: 33).

Jordan (2004) identified the following interaction features when studying teachers involved in co-constructing with children, these features emphasise:

- children as more active in the process of negotiating ideas or activities, for example, children might check things more deliberately with their adult mentors;
- the importance of children learning to check personal understandings against other peoples' and deliberately seeking other's understandings to extend their own knowledge; and
- children learning to manage statements, questions, answers,

comparison, contrast and reflection as the process of learning to learn with and from others.

In both scaffolding and co-construction, a degree of sensitivity to the children's understandings and interests is essential for it to connect with their interests and past experiences.

Developing shared attention

In relation to learning with and from someone, the establishment of joint attention, the negotiation of meaning and an appreciation at some level of each other's' intentions is a key foundation if scaffolding and co-construction are to work. This idea is supported in research by Camaioni (2001), who found a relationship between children's vocabularies and the time invested in joint attention by their mothers. This was also the case where mothers adapted to children's direction of attention, as opposed to mother's directing children's attention to an object, which did not show an association with vocabulary size. In other words practice and experience of using language to guide learning in collaboration develops and hones children's ability to do this effectively.

Example 2

This is one of a series of four observations made in a drop in session for parents and children at an art gallery. Dan, aged 2 years, had spent an extended period each week engaging with slightly varying roller-printing activities. The practitioners facilitating the session noticed his deep engagement with a roller-printing activity and added different textures, colours and tools each week. Each week this has been the first-choice activity for Dan. His mother Gemma had sat alongside him each week.

> Dan spends a couple of minutes applying glue from a pot to paper using a glue spreader, seeing a tray with a roller he leaves the gluing and picks up the roller. Dan rolls the roller against his hand and then movers it slowly from the bottom of the tray gradually towards a line of yellow paint across the top of the tray. As the yellow colour appears on the roller he draws the roller back down the tray watching the tray change from the green background to the yellow colour of the paint. He gives a smaller sponge roller to his mum who is sitting next to him.
> 'Two' says Dan 'that' he adds pointing at the tray.
> She rolls the sponge slowly at right angles to Dan's line and draws his attention to the lines on 'your line of paint' and the dots produced

(Continues)

(Continued)

> by the sponge. Dan takes the roller that is still covered in yellow paint out of the tray and rolls it across an adjacent piece of paper. He takes up a pinch of punched-out paper circles and sprinkles them into the paint tray. He rolls over the paper circles with the roller watching them sticking on to the roller. He sprinkles more circles on to the roller before rolling them onto the paper.

There is much less language involved in this activity due in large part to the age of the child, but perhaps also due to the nature and personality of both parent and child. There is clearly no firm outcome in the adult's mind who is very attentive, focused and happy to respond to Dan's suggestion. Dan is keen for his mother to join in but this is observed through actions rather than words. There is a sense of Dan wanting to share the feeling of the weight of the roller, the stickiness of the paint and glue, and the colour, form and patterns produced by the activity.

⚬━ Key idea: shared thinking

Rogoff (1998) uses the phrase 'shared thinking' to draw attention to an adult and child not just having a mutual understanding but working together to extend that understanding through cooperative reasoning. Rogoff uses this phrase flexibly across a range of interactive styles that might include scaffolding and co-construction:

> Thus collaboration is a process that can take many forms, whether intended or accidental, mutual or one-sided, face to face, shoulder to shoulder, or distant, congenial or contested: the key feature is that in collaboration people are involved in others' thinking processes through shared endeavours. (Rogoff, 1998: 728)

Rogoff argues that 'co-operative learning arrangements promote the use of higher quality cognitive reasoning strategies and metacognitive approaches more than in individual arrangements' (Rogoff, 1998: 717). She emphasises that young children by the age of 2 are already deeply embedded in cultures of shared understanding and that shared thinking need not be verbalised and can be embedded in joint activity and gesture. However, she states that where language is part of the clarification of intentions and understandings 'such interaction may provide both the impetus and resources for children to go beyond their current level of understanding' (Rogoff, 1990: 204). Nevertheless Rogoff suggests that too frequently research focuses on face to face interactions and pays insufficient attention to contextual guidance offered to children by activity. Rogoff (1990) identifies Trevarthen's (1998) conception of intersubjectivity as a central component in the process of the development of shared thinking through the way in which adults and communities guide participation in physical and social activities (see Chapter 1). Rogoff's studies suggest that developing and managing intersubjectivity is a focus of activity in children under the age of 1 year. This is evident in the exchange of expressions, touches and gestures between babies and those they meet. 'I see deliberateness developing over infancy, one of the transformations of intersubjectivity that exists from the start' (Rogoff, 1990: 82).

Children's ability to engage with others by recognising the focus of their gaze and being able to read their intentions, motivations and emotions is a precursor to the collaborative learning processes identified so far. Each joint attention increases children's experiences of what others are likely to be thinking and the more sensitive adults are to this the more they can help children develop their skill in achieving and directing joint attention.

Recommended further reading

Rogoff, B. (1998) 'Cognition as a collaborative process', in D. Kuhn and R.S. Siegler (eds), *Handbook of Child Psychology*. New York: Wiley & Sons.

Developing sustained shared thinking

Chapter 3 made reference to the Researching Effective Pedagogy in the Early Years (REPEY) project (Siraj-Blatchford et al., 2003) which was a part of the larger EPPE Study (Sylva et al., 2010). In this project a sample of settings with the most positive outcomes for children (controlled for starting points and social background) were investigated in more detail. The REPEY view of high-quality interactions contributing to these positive outcomes is illustrated in the following extract:

> The staff clearly enjoyed being with the children and engaged with them in a respectful caring way, without criticism or harshness. They encouraged the children to try new experiences and were very enthusiastic about their efforts. The staff appeared to be constantly aware of looking out for opportunities to scaffold children's learning by inviting children to say what they thought in order to assess their levels of knowledge and understanding. They intervened when they thought it was appropriate but also allowed the children time to explore for themselves. The adult interventions were most often in the form of questions that provoke speculation and extend the imagination. (Siraj-Blatchford et al., 2003: 127)

Siraj-Blatchford defined SST as: 'Episodes, in which two or more individuals work together in an intellectual way to solve a problem, clarify a concept, evaluate activities or extend narratives etc. During periods of sustained shared thinking both parties contribute to the thinking and develop and extend the discourse' (Siraj-Blatchford, 2004: 147).

Siraj-Blatchford (2008) explained how shared thinking might be supported with younger age groups where language exchange was less developed. She identified the following as being potential roles for practitioners to promote SST:

- tuning in to children's interests and showing genuine interest;
- respecting children's decisions and choices;
- inviting children to elaborate on what they are doing and recapping or commentating to clarify their focus of interest;
- offering adult feelings or experiences and joining in alongside or with children; and
- helping children reflect on what they have done and how they might continue.

Many of these features are illustrated in the final example in this chapter.

Example 3

Context: 17-month-old Chloe who is only recently toddling from one place to another, negotiates her activity with her mother, Haley. While Chloe demonstrates her desire to explore water her mother tries to prevent her from getting too wet. The activity takes place in a high-street shop converted into a drop-in playroom.

> Chloe moves over to a large water tray placed on the floor. She has a clear and immediate intention to walk up to and step into the water tray. Haley supports Chloe playing by the tray having removed Chloe's tights so she can paddle. Following persistent attempts by Chloe to sit down in the water tray one of the practitioners brings over a similar size tray filled with pasta. Chloe is initially very upset by this and refuses to approach it. Chloe watches as pasta is poured from a scoop into a jug, she says, 'Want my tea'. Haley repeats this 'You want your tea?'.
>
> Chloe puts her hand into the jug to feel the pasta at the bottom. Chloe sits in the tray of pasta putting handfuls of pasta into the jug. Haley having supported Chloe climbing into the tray tickles Chloe's sides 'I'm right behind you' and she rustles the pasta on either side of Chloe with her fingers. She takes two handful's of pasta and lets them fall gently over Chloe's head 'It's raining', Haley says as Chloe looks up. Haley repeats this and then Chloe sprinkles pasta over her own head. 'Weeeeeee' says Haley, 'Wee' says Chloe. Chloe puts some pasta

into the jug and pretends to drink from it. 'Shall we put some more in?' asks Haley. Chloe tries to lean back 'Do you want to lie down?' 'Yeah, yeah' says Chloe.

Haley and one of the practitioners move the things around to make more space in the tray and Chloe lies back with Haley supporting her head and back. Haley starts explaining to the practitioner how she puts a baby bath on the floor at home for Chloe to play in. As the conversation continues Chloe continues to put pasta into the jug using the scoop. Haley's mobile phone rings and Chloe, in a sitting position, bounces up and down in time with the music, then continues to scoop and pour pasta. Haley returns and tells Chloe that she will pick up the pasta and put it back in the tray. Chloe remains in the tray putting individual pieces of pasta into the jug.

Chloe's interest and motivation to sit in the water is anticipated by her mother who goes as far as she can in helping Chloe to paddle in the water. The offer of being able to sit in a tray of pasta as an alternative is not immediately welcomed by Chloe but she is helped to see the similarities of the flow of the pasta to the flow of the water. In this way, ideas are passed back and forth in the dyad and Chloe pretends to drink the water. Although it is not immediately apparent in the exchange between the parent and child, it is interesting to have the resemblance to the bathing activity at home revealed. This could explain why Haley was so quick to anticipate Chloe's intentions.

During my own research (Needham, 2011), I initially sought to identify examples of sustained shared thinking, co-construction and scaffolding in parent and child sessions. However interactions were often hard to categorise as discreet examples of either scaffolding or co-construction as many blended features of both. The examples offered so far in this chapter have illustrated that features of scaffolding, co-construction and sustained shared thinking are visible with young children within the activities offered in these parent and child groups.

In conducting my research I followed and recorded 20 different children's activities during a morning session and endeavoured to analyse interactions with adults. It seemed that while episodes of activity might be extended, interactions in the sessions were frequently short and oblique, shifting from one mode of engagement into another. Where interactions were more extended they often picked up on recurring themes or children's interests, as with Chloe.

When children were tracked over several sessions sustained shared thinking was seen to occur in discreet time blocks, spread across morning sessions and spread across weeks as in the example of Dan's roller-printing. Research by Hasan (2002) suggests that children may be advantaged when adults involve them in reflection on events over time, that is, connecting the present to similar events in the past or with the future which she refers to as polychronic interactions.

Promoting an awareness of thinking and learning

The analyses of interaction discussed in this chapter draws attention to the importance of helping children to reflect on their learning as it occurs or in review sessions. In doing so children are more able to direct their engagement with activities and set increasingly focused directions for their learning. Metacognition is a word that is often used to refer to the mental processes that reflect on and direct learning. 'The proper exercise of human intelligence is not simply on possessing certain mental tools, but knowing enough about those tools to be able to deploy them effectively and deliberately' (Thornton, 2002: 81).

Thornton draws attention to children as young as 2 years old who show awareness of memory strategies and rehearse the location of hidden objects that they will be asked to retrieve later by repeatedly looking at and pointing to the hiding places of the objects (Thornton, 2002). She suggests that metacognition develops slowly and in gradual stages, with new problem-solving experiences offering the child fresh insight, new awareness and strategies for an iterative learning process.

Researchers such as Bruner (1986) and Camaioni (2001) suggest that while examples of psychological desires are presented by some children before their second birthday, references to beliefs using 'think' and 'know' begin much later, just before the third birthday. Bruner (1986) comments that metacognition appears to vary according to cultural background and can be taught through interaction. He suggests that the beginnings of this awareness can be observed in 'self-corrections in utterances either to bring one's utterances into line with one's intent or to make them comprehensible to an interlocutor' (Bruner, 1986: 67) and that this can be observed as early as 18 months.

The examples presented in this chapter illustrate that within the social framework of parent and child groups, aspects of both scaffolding and co-construction can be used by adults as naturally occurring elements of interactions. Articulating these concepts reminds us that we need to remember the importance of everyday conversations, thinking beyond the immediate task at hand and keeping longer-term attitudes to learning in mind.

The overt agenda within a great deal of adult–child interaction in the early years is around concept formation and language development. The more implicit sub-text, which is sometimes neglected, is about the nature of knowledge and how it is constructed, who accredits knowledge and the child's role in accumulating knowledge. Siraj-Blatchford (2007) suggests that the ongoing arguments about the nature of pedagogies focusing on content rather than process are based on a false dichotomy, because the two things are so closely connected. Discussions too often focus on learning things rather than the processes that accompany them (Siraj-Blatchford, 2007). The research presented in the next chapter investigates the nature and balance of the interactions offered in parent and child groups and the cultures of learning they may evoke.

Cultures of learning

Many of the authors cited in this chapter, (Bruner, 1986; Camaioni, 2001; Rogoff, 1998; Thornton, 2002) draw particular attention to the problems associated with child development theories that are based upon data collected mostly from middle-class European and European American families, often in controlled conditions. They also express concern that age guides to development vary considerably between individuals and cultures, and call for more information to be gathered in relation to different cultures' and subcultures' approaches to interactions.

Rogoff (1998) draws attention to a number of studies involving different age groups, including 7-month-olds, illustrating that the notion of contingent scaffolding, which is matched to the level of the child and faded out as the child assumes greater control, appears to be a common phenomenon across many middle-class mothers from different nations. Rogoff's work argues that by looking at cultural comparisons of activity these debated issues regarding the application of cognition to younger children become much clearer.

Rogoff also traced wide variations in the degree to which adults join in with and agree roles with children in play. She notes that in some communities play is considered a child's domain (Rogoff et al., 1998), but even in some middle-class communities where adults acted as playmates with young children they were likely to take differing roles than child companions in play. 'Dunn and Dale (1984) found that the play of two year-olds with their older siblings commonly involved the close meshing of the partners in complementary pretend roles. Whereas mothers generally observed and supported play without entering it by performing pretend roles and actions' (Rogoff, 1998: 709).

Individuals' attitudes to learning are governed by cultural expectations, practices and resources, as well as personal individual dispositions. Brooker (2002) illustrated the potential differences in attitudes towards early education between different parents and practitioners showing how some parents expected early education experiences to be more formal and less play centred. Different situations afford greater and fewer opportunities for development and these opportunities are mediated by the way adults interact with children within them. It is not that every interaction counts but the weight of experience may begin to tell over time in the shape of children's thinking about thinking.

Throughout this book we argue that the nature and tone of everyday interactions shape language, thought action and then dispositions, phrases, patterns of thinking and speaking that will facilitate learning in partnership with others. We also emphasise that the emotional, cognitive and metacognitive are interconnected, that development begins from birth, and that while the process may be natural, routine and taken for granted it is not, therefore, always carefully reflected upon. From our experiences in the English and Australian contexts, dual-focused groups are potentially ideal for raising adults' and children's awareness of a range of ways of being and learning individually, collaboratively and collectively. We suggest elsewhere (Needham and Jackson, 2014) that this more open and co-constructive approach to parent support might be more suited to many parents, compared with more directed parenting courses. Chapter 8 explores the learning cultures in two dual-focus groups in more detail.

Finally, parent and child groups provide a forum to witness different styles of interaction and a place to reflect on these unconsciously and consciously, implicitly through personal reflection or in dialogue with others. We also need to keep in mind the nature of interactions between practitioners, children and parents in relation to issues of power and knowledge. We need to continually reflect on our expectations of children and parents and the role of the state in intervening in parent–child relationships (Vandenbroeck et al., 2009).

Reflective activities: parents and practitioners as co-researchers

The terms scaffolding and co-construction are helpful in fostering an awareness of interactions that support the development of children's experience of thinking with others and for themselves and there are a number of additional helpful features raised by considering shared thinking. Figure 7.1 summarises these three areas and suggests their potential to overlap and interplay in interaction.

Try using the elements in Figure 7.1 to review the Chloe example and consider which features you think are present in the interaction. Discuss your analysis of the example with a partner. You might try repeating this activity with an example from your own experience.

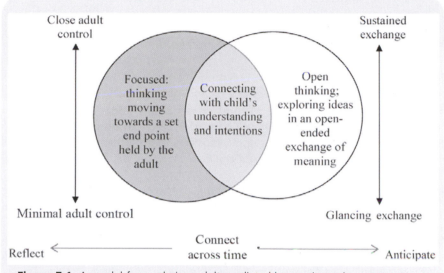

Figure 7.1 A model for analysing adult-mediated interaction using open, focused and reflective shared thinking regulated by adult control and timing

References

Athey, C. (2007) *Extending Thought in Young Children*. London: Sage.

Brooker, L. (2002) *Starting School: Young Children Learning Cultures*. Buckingham: Open University Press.

Bruner, J. (1986) *Actual Minds, Possible Worlds*. [online] Cambridge, MA: Harvard University Press.

Camaioni, L. (2001) 'Early language', in G.J. Bremner and A. Fogel (eds), *Blackwell Handbook of Infant Development*. Malden, MA: Blackwell.

Greenfield, P. (1984) 'Theory of the teacher in learning activities', in B. Rogoff and J. Lave (eds), *Everyday Cognition*. Cambridge, MA: Harvard University Press.

Hasan, R. (2002) 'Semiotic mediation and mental development in pluralistic societies; some implications for tomorrow's schooling', in G. Wells and G. Claxton (eds), *Learning for Life in the 21st Century*. Oxford: Blackwell.

Hohmann, M. and Weikart, D.P. (2002) *Educating Young Children*. Yipsilanti, MI: High Scope Press.

Jordan, B. (2004) 'Scaffolding learning and co-constructing understandings', in A. Anning, J. Cullen and M. Fleer (eds), *Early Childhood Studies*. London: Paul Chapman Publishing.

MacNaughton, G. (2003) *Shaping Early Childhood: Learners, Curriculum and Context*. Maidenhead: Open University Press.

Needham, M. (2011) 'Learning to learn in supported parent and toddler groups: a sociocultural investigation', PhD thesis, London University, London.

Needham, M. and Jackson, D. (2014) 'It ain't what you do, it's the way that you do it!', in M. Reed and R. Walker (eds), *Early Childhood Studies: A Critical Companion*.

Rogoff, B. (1990) *Apprenticeship Thinking in the Social Context*. New York: Open University Press.

Rogoff, B. (1998) 'Cognition as a collaborative process', in D. Kuhn and R.S. Siegler (eds), *Handbook of Child Psychology*. New York: Wiley & Sons.

Rogoff, B., Mosier, C., Mystry, J. and Göncü, A. (1998) *Toddlers' Guided Participation with Caregivers in Cultural Activity*. London: Routledge.

Schweinhart, L.J., Montie, J., Xiang, Z., Barnett, W.S., Belfield, C.R. and Nores, M. (2005) *Finding of the Perry Preschool Programme Through to Age 40*. Ypsilanti, MI: HighScope Press.

Siraj-Blatchford, I. (2004) 'Quality teaching in the early years', in A. Anning, J. Cullen and M. Fleer (eds), *Early Childhood Studies*. London: Paul Chapman Publishing.

Siraj-Blatchford, I. (2007) 'Creativity, communication and collaboration: the identification of pedagogic progression in sustained shared thinking', *Asia Pacific Journal of Research in Early Childhood Education*, 1(2): 3–23.

Siraj-Blatchford, I. (2008) 'Promoting adult pedagogy and child learning in the Early Years Foundation Stage', *Promoting Diversity*. [online]. University of Wolverhampton, 21.2.2008.

Siraj-Blatchford, I., Taggart, B., Sammons, P. and Elliot, K. (2003) *Intensive Case Studies of Practice Across the Foundation Stage*. [online] London: Institute of Education. p. 168.

Sylva, K., Melhuish, E., Sammons, P., Siraj-Blatchford, I. and Taggart, B. (2010) *Early Childhood Matters Evidence from the Effective Pre-School and Primary Education Project*. London: Routledge.

Thornton, S. (2002) *Growing Minds*. Basingstoke: Palgrave MacMillan.

Trevarthen, C. (1998) 'The child's need to learn a culture', in M. Woodhead, D. Faulkner and L. Karen (eds), *Cultural Worlds of Early Childhood*. London: Routledge.

Vandenbroeck, M., Boonaert, T., Van Der Mespel, S. and De Brabandere, K. (2009) 'Dialogical spaces to reconceptualize parent support in the social investment state', *Contemporary Issues in Early Childhood*, 10(1): 66–77.

Weikart, D.P., Bond, J.T. and J.T., N. (1978) *The Ypsilanti Perry Pre-school Project: Pre-school Years and Longitudinal Results Through Fourth Grade*. [online] Ypsilanti, Mich: HighScope Educational Research Foundation.

Wood, D. (1998) *How Children Think and Learn*. [online] Oxford: Blackwell.

Wood, D., Bruner, J.C. and Ross, G. (1976) 'The role of tutoring in problem solving', *Journal of Child Psychology and Psychiatry*, 17: 89–100.

Wylie, C. and Thompson, J. (2003) 'The long-term contribution of early childhood education to children's performance – evidence from New Zealand', *International Journal of Early Years Education*, 11(1): 69–78.

CHAPTER 8

Learning to play together

Chapter overview

This chapter explores the nature and range of interaction in two case study dual-focused groups in England. It explores the learning culture engendered during the activities experienced by a sample of 12 children aged 18 months to 4 years split across the two groups. The chapter illustrates how systematic observation and coding of data can be used to support comparison and to develop insights into the experiences of children. The narrative observations and the model of interaction, already outlined in Chapter 7, were used to develop a pictorial representation of the patterns of interaction that were encountered in the two parent and child groups.

Presenting case studies

Case studies can be very powerful tools for revealing detailed examples of how issues and practices manifest themselves in particular situations. They can be helpful in raising topics for reflection and debate but it is dangerous to draw generalisations from them. The aim of the study which developed the case studies presented in this chapter (Needham, 2011) was to identify and analyse the patterns of interaction that occurred between adults and children in order to consider the implications of these experiences for children's learning.

Each child's learning story was divided into episodes on the basis of related materials, actions and intentions such as playing with a particular set of objects, playing in a particular location or continuing a play theme. These episodes were then analysed using the model for regulating shared thinking presented in Chapter 7 (Figure 7.1). We begin by comparing the individual elements of the coding framework before reflecting in more detail on how these elements are combined into modes of interaction. The initial analysis of the individual elements of the coding framework provides a useful starting point for comparing activity across the two case study groups.

Figure 8.1 presents the number of episodes in each setting that were coded using the elements of the model for regulating shared thinking. The straightforward comparison of the codes allocated in each of the case study settings highlights many similarities and only a few differences between the two settings, which are referred to here as Outwell and Talktime.

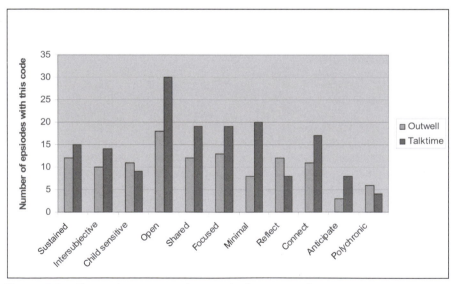

Figure 8.1 Comparing category frequencies by case study group

The Outwell case study was a practitioner-led outreach group from a children's centre which offered a two-and-a-quarter-hour morning session for up to 20 families in a church hall. Talktime offered a two-hour morning session for up to 15 families in a children's centre including a 20 to 30 minute discussion time.

Although there was a higher frequency of episodes in the Talktime group a similar pattern of distribution of frequency occurred across both groups. The timing of the groups was similar but a greater number of episodes were recorded in the Talktime setting. This might have been because of the greater range of activities available in the Talktime group which was located in a purpose-built, dedicated room within a children's centre. The permanent layout of the Talktime group with materials openly accessible to the children, presented them with greater options not only in terms of individual activities but for transferring equipment between locations in the room.

The 51 to 33 difference in the number of episodes recorded between the groups is interesting because there was a similar structure and scope for exploratory and creative play in both groups. The pattern of data analysis initially suggests that while the Talktime group as a whole experienced a greater number of episodes, the pattern of elements were in proportion with this difference. It also suggests that the episodes in the Outwell group were on average longer in nature.

The most prominent feature in Figure 8.1 is the higher frequency of open-ended interactions compared with focused interactions, particularly in the Talktime group. This pattern of interaction is similar to Rogoff's finding that in play learning contexts adults tend to give control of the learning context over to the child: 'mothers generally observed and supported the play without entering it by performing pretend roles and actions' (Rogoff et al., 1998: 709).

Some of the elements of the four reflective metacognitions on the right of Figure 8.1 suggest differences between the groups with regard to the frequency that adults encourage children to 'reflect' on events and connect events across time (polychronic). These two elements of inter-action run counter to the otherwise similar pattern in the other categories. The higher number of episodes with these codes in the Outwell group suggests a parallel with other research study findings that show that higher frequencies of reflective interaction containing 'reflection' and 'connection of events over time' may occur in cultural groups with more educational qualifications, irrespective of ethnicity (Hasan, 2002; Rogoff et al., 1998). The Outwell group contained four graduates among the six parents sampled, while the Talktime group had no graduate parents. The data should not be used to draw conclusions about the interactive styles of the parents, it is too limited in time and location, but it does illustrate the potential of dual focus groups to widen repertoires of practice.

Modes of adult–child interaction

The next phase of the analysis of the case studies examined separate episodes and identified the patterns of elements from the analytical framework in order to identify how they were combined into modes of interaction. This process led to the identification of the following modes of interaction: controlling, monitoring and affirming, directing learning, sharing ideas and playing, which are described in the following sections of the chapter.

Controlling

Some episodes of activity were blankly coded because they focused on controlling or meeting the needs of a situation for example when children needed to go to the toilet, put on an apron, or wipe their nose. These episodes prioritised close control over the elements of collaborative mediation because they were not open to supporting the child's own interests or serving a deliberate learning objective of the parent. That is not to say that the ways in which these episodes are managed are not important because they may serve to regulate the way that children feel about the level of control and voice that they should anticipate in relationships.

Monitoring and affirming

As in the supported play groups (Chapter 6) there were relatively few episodes where children were occupied on their own or with other children completely independently from adults. However in the majority of episodes the adult role was to monitor or observe the activity. Interactions in the 'monitoring support' mode were characterised by adults being present, watchful, giving space to children's activities and acting to conserve and prolong them with minimal disruption. In these activities adults were present but, for the most part, quiet and did not intervene unless children required support.

These episodes were coded as containing only minimal or momentary connections or containing both open and minimal connections. The adults did sometimes offer minimal support which might be silent in order to ensure that the child could continue, thereby identifying some idea of what children were trying to achieve and supporting their intention.

In the example which follows, Abas's mother, Serena, offers a sequence of musical instruments that prolongs his activity of testing them but there is little exchange between the two regarding the quality of each instrument. Serena appeared to be particularly concerned that he share the resources fairly with those around him and not damage them. There was also a slight tension in the activity with a sense that she might respond by asserting control at any moment.

Monitoring: Abas, age 30 months, with his mother

Abas hears a child on the carpeted area banging a drum. He looks around and then moves towards them taking off the apron and passing it to his mum who is already helping him to take it off. The mums on the carpet arrange the drums to make space for Abas and his mother. Abas and Kerry [child] take it in turns to bang on a large low drum with beaters.

'Share it,' says mum. The children continue.

'Share it,' they are advised again.

Abas starts trying to move the drum to his advantage.

'Share,' says his mum and offers him a different drum from the basket of instruments which he places next to him and then beats slowly and deliberately. Mum offers him a shaker from the basket which she shakes and then he copies her briefly and then uses the shaker as a beater to continue beating the drum as before. Mum offers him a transparent layered shaker with beads that she revolves so he can hear the sound and see the beads moving inside. Abas takes the shaker and lays it beside himself. Mum offers him a set of sleigh bells which he shakes and lays aside. Mum then offers him a toy hand-bell from a set of hand-bells as Iona starts to ring two bells from the same set and dance in time as she rings them. Abas takes the offered bell and uses it to hit the drum several times. He then stands up to copy Iona and accepts a second offered bell. He turns around to look at himself in a full length mirror that is next to him. He rings the bells one by one and then reverses to sit on his mother's lap and slides down onto the floor in front of her giving one bell to her and offering the other to Kerry.

This example demonstrates the potential to become a completely controlling episode and contrasts with the other examples where Abas's mother was more relaxed and feeds Abas's own activity. She offers minimal input which may help to sustain the activity and offer control and self-confidence to the child but it does not develop or extend beyond the child's zone of proximal development. In this mode, reflection on any knowledge gained seems to be left entirely to the child unless the activity is returned to in later conversations or episodes.

In 'affirming support' activities the adults were observing the children's activities and commenting on what they were doing such as 'That is nice, oh you did it', or asking rhetorical questions such as, 'Are you putting the hat on'? The following example of the affirming mode centres on Maisy who was not quite 2 years old. She was capable of developing imaginary play scenarios in other episodes and is identified as such by her mother, who links this to having two older siblings. In this example, Maisy's mother and the setting staff play a supporting role. They offer support and prompting questions that affirm their support for Maisy's activity. This affirms Maisy as the focus of attention and places the child at the centre of activity pursuing interests. Such exchanges affirm roles where adults pose questions and support the children. While in one way this places control with children, it also sets limited flexibility around the role adults play and restricts children's power to engage them in playful modes and assign them new roles.

Affirming: Maisy, age 21 months, with Mum

Maisy takes a policewoman's hat from one of three boxes of dressing-up clothes. She puts it on and her mum encourages her to move around the other side of the boxes to look at herself in the mirror. Having looked at herself briefly in the mirror, Maisy places the hat on a table by the boxes and then starts to pull items from the box as if considering their appeal. She holds up a yellow belt and her mum says 'It's a Bob the builder belt for putting tools in'. She lays the belt on the floor and takes out a pink dress which her mum helps her to put on over her clothes. A practitioner from the centre passing through the room stops and says how beautiful the dress looks and how it matches with Maisy's pink shoes.

Maisy pulls out a blue silky dress and starts to take off the pink dress giving the blue dress to her mother to hold. Maisy pulls out a pair of adult's heeled sandals from the box and sits down to put them on, again mum helps her to do this. Having put on the shoes she starts to move slowly across the non-carpeted part of the room towards the toilets looking and listening to the clicks of the shoes on the floor. Before she reaches the toilets she turns around and comes back to her mother, walking up close to her and putting her face close up to her mother's with a broad smile, using her eyes to engage her mother. She walks back towards the toilets and back to her mother and then her mother helps her to put on the blue dress. They exchange some quiet words during this process. Maisy walks towards the toilets once again, this time holding up the hem of the dress so that she can look at her feet. [Maisy's mum says to Martin that she loves dressing up at the moment]. Maisy moves up to Kay [practitioner] to show her the dress.

'Is this Cinderella then mum?' Kay says to Maisy and her mother. 'Where are you going now?'

In this mode, responsibility for reflecting on the activity is predominantly left with the child but the adult has acknowledged the value of the activity and possibly drawn attention to particular elements of the activity such as characterisation in the first example or sound-making in the second. It is difficult to see these monitoring and affirming modes as collaborative learning: the learning is turned over to the child and the adult offers only a small amount of spoken feedback as long as the child is keeping within the bounds of expected behaviour. The adult may see things from the child's point of view but thinking is not shared between the adult and child and there is little co-construction of meaning. It could be argued that these episodes are creating a scaffold for reflection on experience by creating a space for promoting the value of individual exploration. This may be true but it does not match with the descriptions of scaffolding offered in Chapter 7 (Jordan, 2004; Wood, 1998). Monitoring and affirming episodes were not perceived to be intersubjective and so rarely contained elements of metacognitive support. This perhaps reflects a lack of direct engagement between adult and child rather than any insensitivity.

Directing learning

These episodes featured the 'focus' element from the analytical framework but not the 'open' or 'minimal' elements. They varied in nature depending on how well the adult's strategy connected with the child's interest. There were several examples where the adult seemed intent on the transmission of a particular point irrespective of connection with the child's needs. These directed learning modes can therefore be subdivided into two types, depending on the sensitivity of the adult to the child's ability to engage with the activity. The apparently more successful examples of 'directing learning' episodes feature shared agenda-setting and intersubjectivity. The apparently less successful attempts at direct learning lacked the shared direction and seemed to lack intersubjectivity. These episodes also emphasised the power of the child to accept or reject the direction offered by the adult and demonstrate that the child may choose to reject what the adult is proposing or may simply not understand what the adult is offering.

In the two examples that follow there is an implicit requirement on the child to anticipate the adult's intention and connect labels with objects in the here and now. In the first example Ahmed appears to be motivated initially to explore the texture and control of the water in combination with the objects set out with it. His mother identifies the opportunities for developing shared labels for the shaped objects in the water and seems to initiate a familiar 'game' format. Ahmed is clearly able to respond correctly to his mother's requests, a degree of intersubjectivity is established and the activity is sustained for several exchanges. Ahmed's acceptance of the game offered by his mother contrasts with Iona's rejection of the offered discourse in the second example.

Directing learning (type 1 accepted): Ahmed, age 15 months, with his mother

As soon as they arrive, mum asks if the water activity is still going on. Mum helps Ahmed to find an apron and to put it on. He stands by a pan in which an older child has placed a waterwheel. His mother holds his hand and guides him, pouring water from a small blue cup over the waterwheel. Ahmed smiles broadly as the water flows over the wheel making it spin around. His mother continues to support this for several minutes and then Ahmed continues to spin the wheel using his hand. Ahmed struggles to reach inside the pan to the shapes and containers inside. He takes the shapes and passes them to his mum. She asks for the star and draws his attention to the star by holding it out to show him saying, 'Good boy'. Ahmed seems to share the connection between this word and the yellow star-shaped pastry cutter in the water.

'Star chaieya,' [can I have the star please] says his mum.

Ahmed picks out the star again from a red bowl next to the pan.

'Cross chaieya … Hexagon chaieya' says mum.

As he hands her the objects, she shows them to him and names them.

'Ahmed Star chaieya. Star'.

'Star' says Ahmed handing his mother the star.

'Good boy,' she says smiling enthusiastically.

There are several shapes in a red bowl that mum offers to Ahmed. She asks him to picks objects from the bowl.

'Square dedo.' [pass the square] 'Hexagon dedo. Cup dedo. Ysme [this thing] dedo,' she says as Ahmed passes the objects from the bowl and drops them into the pan. Again, when she says 'star dedo' Ahmed selects the appropriate shape and she smiles and says good boy. 'Missed,' she says as the object that Ahmed is dropping back into the pan misses and lands on the floor. He picks up the cup and gives it a tentative lick.

'Ne ne [no no],' says mum.

Ahmed cannot now reach the objects in the bottom of the pan and Martin helps mum to move the pan to a chair so Ahmed can see inside.

Ahmed's mother explained her role in the following way: 'I try to make it as interactive as possible. He can't sit still and listen to a story; you have to involve him, he is at the age where he likes to feel involved.' This suggests that she identifies a proactive role for herself in involving Ahmed with the materials as she perceives they should be used. She identifies knowledge for acquisition explicitly to Ahmed and reviews the extent to which he has absorbed that knowledge.

In the second example Iona seems content in controlling the objects going into and out of the bucket. As in the previous episode featuring Ahmed, Iona's mother seeks to initiate a familiar game allocating number names to a controlled counting process. On this occasion however Iona very clearly rejects this offer and creates a space between herself and her mother to pursue her own preferred agenda. Iona's rapid and decisive action suggests that she is very aware of what her mother is trying to achieve and indicates clearly it is not what she wants to do right now.

Directing learning (type 2 not accepted): Iona, age 21 months, with her mother

Iona returns to the chalkboard and stands next to Fazal [child]. She wipes the board from side to side with a wooden board duster. She picks up the bucket from the stand and moves away from the easel. Iona takes the bucket to the middle of the carpet area where there are corks and tamarind seeds in metal bowls. 'Shall we put the corks into the bucket?' asks her mum. They begin to fill the bucket with corks one by one.

'Shall we count them?' asks her mum, '1 … 2 … 3' '1 … 2 … 3'.

Iona moves the bucket a couple of feet away from her mum and puts the corks in handfuls into the bucket. Iona says 'bye,' and waves to her mum. She moves to the home corner and watches Jack, who has a bucket and a wooden spoon.

It is easy to imagine a similar situation where understanding was simply not present, in which the child would continue without reacting at all to the mother's initiative. The first example of 'directed learning' does carry features of a more collaborative learning dialogue, with ideas exchanged and in some cases sustained between the adult and child, but the adult is clearly in charge of the direction that the thinking is taking. This creates a scaffold in the sense that Jordan (2004) invokes where the child has less practice in pursuing a particular agenda and is probing the thoughts of the learning partner.

Sharing ideas

Episodes in this category featured the shared and open elements from the analytical framework. They were also intersubjective and there was more of a tendency compared to the previous modes for the adult support to be adjusted. The adults offered more or less support and focus depending on their perception of the child's need for support. The adult support might be faded out, enabling the child to pursue her or his own independent enquiry, or increased. This fits most closely with the notion of scaffolding described by Wood (1998), because it builds upon the child's initiative but the adult support leads towards a particular point that the adult considers appropriate to the child and the materials.

This mode also seemed more likely to include metacognitive elements. The following examples illustrate a clearer shared purpose as compared to some of the previous modes of interaction. In this first example the activity has been set out by the practitioner, Yasmeen, and she is working together with Rona (age 22 months) to achieve a defined but flexible outcome.

In the following example producing a food item is the clear function of the activity. This is clear to Rona and she is eager to engage with the process of making the nest and with eating several of the components. The process of making the nest is transferred as much as possible to Rona. The practitioner, Yasmeen, consistently offers prompts to the next step but is not overly controlling on quantities or layout. She invites children to consider their feelings and offers them vocabulary to express actions and feelings.

Sharing ideas: Rona, age 22 months, with practitioner Yasmeen

Rona, having arrived and taken off her coat, moves straight to the activity table, which is set out with an eye-catching patterned tablecloth. Yasmeen asks Rona if she would like to make an Easter nest. Rona nods, smiles, and sits down at the table. Yasmeen provides Rona with an empty bowl and asks if she would like some of the mix. 'We can squeeze honey in and then mix it up.' She offers Rona a small dish with pieces of shredded wheat, a bowl with mixed raisins and asks again if she would like some. Rona takes small handfuls of the ingredients and puts then into a breakfast bowl. Yasmeen holds the squeezable honey bottle over the bowl and they both squeeze some honey into the bowl.

'Mix it up Rona! Mix Mix Mix,' says Yasmeen. 'Rona look,' says Yasmeen taking the mixture, which is now bound together. 'Then we can put it in a paper case' Yasmeen continues, offering Rona a paper cake cup. 'Scoop it in, use your fingers to mix it up'.

Rona mixes it some more.

'Have you tasted it? What does it taste like?'

Rona tries a little and smiles broadly at Yasmeen.

'Would you like to put an Easter egg on top?'

Rona takes an egg from the centre of the table and holds it close looking at Yasmeen. 'Put it on top,' says Yasmeen.

Rona continues to look at Yasmeen and shakes her head. 'I know what you're thinking,' says Yasmeen pausing and smiling, 'put it on there and take another one. They are for later'.

Rona quickly complies with this request and puts two of the mini eggs wrapped in foil on top of her nest.

'Do you want to taste this?' Yasmeen asks taking some of the unprocessed shredded wheat herself.

Rona takes a piece and cautiously tries it. 'Crunchy crunch,' says Yasmeen,

> Rona smiles and then picks up a few raisins, trying one.
> 'Do you want to taste another one?' asks Yasmeen.
> Rona shakes her head. She takes some more shredded wheat.
> 'What does it taste like? … Crunchy crunch crunch,' continues Yasmeen.
> Rona smiles and nods.

The first stage of the episode was coded as directing learning but in the second half of the episode the activity switched from constructing the Easter nest to checking out the ingredients. The interaction was more flexible than in the directed learning examples and although Rona did not say anything, there is the sense of a constant exchange of gestures and meanings between the two, which Yasmeen checked by vocalising ideas for Rona to validate.

This particular example appears to have some affinity with Jordan's (2004) description of scaffolding: the activity is pre-planned by the practitioner with a specific outcome in mind. However, it also contains some co-construction of meaning around responses to the experience and guided participation in terms of being inducted and orientated into the process by the adult. This illustrates the difficulty of making distinctions between scaffolding and co-construction in practice. It is clear in the above episode that some elements of control, direction and power remain with the child and that the episode is sustained and extended through dialogue, reflecting sustained shared thinking.

Playing

Finally there were a small number of activities which were shared, open and focused with sustained adult support and intersubjectivity that was not faded out. The examples captured by this coding are different from the other examples of mediating activity because they are less focused on an objective and feature more joint activity and shared enjoyment of the materials.

Vivian, an experienced early years teacher visited the Outwell group regularly to deliver 15-minutes story sessions on behalf of the library service. Vivian chose to spend part of her time getting to know the children. In the following example she was lying on the ground next to Jacob and adopted a playful and excited tone rather than a calm supportive adult mode. Jacob, who was not quite 2 years old and not yet in a position to negotiate the play verbally, engaged enthusiastically with this mode of interaction with which he appeared familiar and confident. The playful activity quickly drew in other adults and children and the exchange promoted swift and urgent reflection on the information exchanged between the participants. Vivian seemed tuned into the excitement and immediacy of this activity for the child, and the other adults seemed to respond to Jacob's enjoyment and Vivian's lead. In this mode the child is at the centre of a group, engaging with other adults and children with a high stake in what transpires.

Playing: Jacob, age 18 months, with Mum and practitioner Vivian

He moves towards the ball again. 'Have you found your ball?' asks mum.

Jacob goes carefully under one in a line of chairs to retrieve the ball but as he touches it, it rolls further along the line of chairs.

'Oh, oh!' says Jacob.

'Oh, oh!' say both adults.

'Can you get it?' says Vivian. 'Where is it? Look?'

Vivian pushes the ball back to Jacob. 'Get it quick, here.'

It passes Jacob and goes under another chair on an adjacent wall. 'Get it quick' says Vivian. 'Have you got it? Where has it gone?'

'Eea, eah eah, eee' Jacob says smiling and laughing, looking at Vivian as he throws the ball back.

'Have you found it?' asks his mum.

'Where is it, where has it gone?' says Vivian rolling it under a chair again. 'Go and fetch it Jacob.'

'Eeah!'

'Where has it gone?' says mum.

'Where is it now?' says Vivian.

His mum comments that he has a ball at home but he doesn't have nearly as much fun with it.

Jacob goes to retrieve the ball again from under a chair.

'Don't bump your head,' says Angela [Rona's grandma].

'Mind your head Jacob,' says mum too, 'Oh oh'.

'Dow!' says Jacob.

'Down down,' says mum. 'Do you want to look at this truck book? You've got one like this at home'.

Jacob continues to try to reach the ball.

Vivian collects and rolls the ball to Jacob but it rolls past and goes under another chair.

'Eeema, Eema,' says Jacob as Vivian helps Jacob to retrieve the ball.

Rona [age 2], who has been watching the game, picks up the ball and bounces it on the floor.

Jacob picks it up. Rona points to the ball and moves closer until she is touching it with her pointing finger. Jacob begins to look concerned and holds on tightly. Angela clears a space to allow the children to throw it to each other and Mum urges Jacob to roll it to his friend.

'Say Jacob,' Angela says to Rona 'Can Jacob roll it to Rona?'

Jacob bounces it to Rona and then moves to sit next to his younger brother on his mother's lap.

🔑 Key idea: play as an activity format

Play gives rise to the opportunity to gain insight into how others perceive the world. This example of the playing mode exhibited features of sustained shared thinking in the playful exchange between participants. It suggests that when adults value activities to such an extent that they join in on similar terms to the children, that they are then more affected by the information offered by the children. The richness of this play example supports the value of thinking of play as an activity format rather than as an activity in its own right (Van Oers, 2010). Learning to play with others enables children to engage more deeply with socially generated knowledge which extends personally generated knowledge.

Van Oers (2010) uses the concept of activity to suggest that play is not an activity of itself but rather a socially developed *activity format* where rules are relaxed and there is more flexibility, and a high level of engagement and personal involvement. This is a very helpful and significant suggestion which challenges the orthodoxy of play as used in everyday language as something frivolous or unimportant. This proposal implies that playing is a format that individuals can benefit from learning to exploit in the context of many activities as a tool to support learning and understanding. Thus play is powerful because creates an intense engagement in the child, which has no clearly defined 'closed' outcome so that it offers children the chance to negotiate play roles, rules and goals so that the end point is less important than the satisfaction gained from the process of developing cognitive and physical mastery(Moyles, 2010).

Hakkarainen (1999, p.234) argues that play as an activity type aims at the mastery of mastering. Play does not produce any concrete knowledge of mastering. It produces general flexibility and a disposition to change one's approach when facing the concrete demands of the situation.

Play is an activity which potentially offers children an opportunity to engage with objects and ideas, to learn about themselves and the wider world, free of some of the physical and social risks of real activity. Present day human activity can be less visible to many children as compared to previous generations who played in family workshops ,homes and fields alongside working family members (Rogoff, 2003). Play in 'modern' society is an increasingly symbolic space, with many toys being abstract objects of investigations or for the re-enactment of second hand fantasy screen experiences. In such a situation access to meaning can be compromised, because the tools require social interpretation and physicality to give them meaning (Rogoff, 2003). Play offers children an important space to make more visceral sense of the world around them.

(Continues)

(Continued)

Recommended further reading

Van Oers, B. (2010) 'Children's enculturation through play', in L. Brooker and
S. Edwards (eds), *Engaging Play*. Maidenhead: Open University Press.

An overview of children's experience of interactions with practitioners in the case studies

The staff in both case study settings were, unsurprisingly, recorded as engaging in fewer interactions with individual children than were the children's parents. Parents remained close to their children through most of the sessions and the practitioners supported different children at different times. The clear variation in the number of recorded interactions between staff and children in the two groups presented in Figure 8.2 is primarily because there was always one more staff member in the Talktime group.

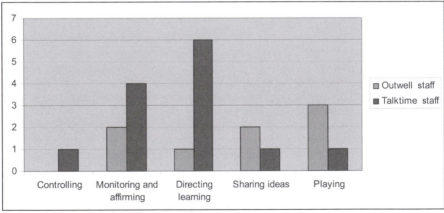

Figure 8.2 Comparing the frequency of the modes of interaction used by staff as experienced by the children in the two case study groups

Outwell began with two practitioners and reduced to one, Talktime started with three and reduced to two, which accounts for the greater frequency of interactions overall in Figure 8.2. The pattern of modes of interaction across Figure 8.2 also suggests that the Talktime staff operated more in terms of observing and supporting children's activity with parents, while the Outwell staff seemed to lead more in planned activities and therefore engaged more frequently in open-ended exchanges with the children. This reflects two slightly different approaches to the practitioner role and shows a tension between facilitating and modelling modes that practitioners need to balance. As Rogoff (2003) points out, interactions are a joint product and it is possible that the children in the Outwell group were more open to more co-constructive exchanges through similar engagement with their parents. More detailed investigations of how the same children and adults respond in different parent and toddler groups could provide interesting clarifications of these questions and help practitioners develop different approaches with different families. By identifying the balance of modes of interaction we begin to create a forum for discussion, reflection and change.

The example of adults 'playing with children' included as an exemplar in this chapter features a practitioner because, as Figure 8.3 demonstrates, there were fewer examples of parents engaging in playing. There was only one example of an adult entering into more imaginative playful behaviour (Moyles, 2010) as compared to exploratory play, and this would suggest that playing in front of other adults is perhaps a significant barrier to play in a public space. However, the richness in this example in terms of emotional and intellectual engagement also suggests that practitioners could enable these play interactions as a more prominent feature of the learning culture within the sessions. The rarity of such playful behaviour in parents was expressed in the comment from Yasmeen, a practitioner at the Outwell group: 'I know, she kind of like jumped in didn't she! I remember seeing her I think wow she is jumping like a frog, but then I know her background and she is used to doing drama, she is not afraid to jump like a frog so that was really nice.'

Parents' modes of interaction

Comparing the frequency with which the different modes were employed by the sample of parents, once again reveals a very similar pattern in the two case study groups. The findings presented in Figure 8.3 suggest that in the context of the case study groups parents co-constructed meanings to a lesser extent than the practitioners. This may reflect socially located attitudes and expectations related to learning in this social space, influenced by the setting they are attending.

If parents' intentions for learning are directed more towards supporting children's personal exploration and offering direct instruction in these groups, which interviews suggested they were, then modelling, discussion or alternative activities might increase opportunities for open exchanges of ideas with parents about the range of opportunities presented by the group. Pramling-Samuelsson and Fleer (2009: 188), in the educare context, assert that 'the teachers can never interact and communicate too much with the toddlers in early childhood education since there are so many children and few adults'. This is less the case in dual-focused groups because adult to child ratios are so high, but the proportion of time adults spent in a less-engaged role in these case study groups suggests this worthy of monitoring, reflection and investigation.

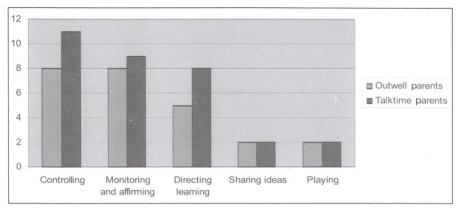

Figure 8.3 Comparing the frequency of the modes of interaction used by parents in the two case study groups

〰️ Reflective activities: modes of interaction

This chapter has illustrated how qualitative observation and coded analysis can be used to reflect on the learning culture present in settings. It can also be used to reflect on the experiences of individual children and adult–child pairings.

Figure 8.4 presents an overview of the reflective elements experienced by three different children. Consider what this suggests about the contrasting experiences of the three children in the parent and child group sessions. How might you respond to these findings if you were the practitioner in this setting?

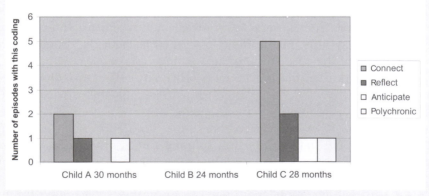

Figure 8.4 Comparing the metacognitive elements of interaction experienced by three selected children

You might try tracking a child across a session or part of one of your own group sessions and try to identify the nature of the interactions that they are experiencing. With a co-worker, compare your interpretations and opinions about how this might inform modelling of interactions or discussions with parents. If you were seeking to affirm parent and child engagement, what things might you draw attention to?

References

Hakkarainen, P. (1999) 'Play and Motivation', in Y. Engestrom, R. Meittinen, R.J. Puna-maki (eds), *Perspectives on Activity Theory*. Cambridge: Cambridge University Press.

Hasan, R. (2002) 'Semiotic mediation and mental development in pluralistic societies; some implications for tomorrow's schooling', in G. Wells and G. Claxton (eds), *Learning for Life in the 21st Century*. Oxford: Blackwell.

Jordan, B. (2004) 'Scaffolding learning and co-constructing understandings', in A. Anning, J. Cullen and M. Fleer (eds), *Early Childhood Studies*. London: Paul Chapman Publishing.

Moyles, J. (2010) *The Excellence of Play*. Maidenhead: Open University Press.

Needham, M. (2011) 'Learning to learn in supported parent and toddler groups: a sociocultural investigation', PhD. thesis London University, London.

Pramling-Samuelsson, I. and Fleer, M. (2009) *Play and Learning in Early Childhood Settings*. Fankston: Springer.

Rogoff, B. (2003) *The Cultural Nature of Human Development*. Oxford: Oxford University Press.

Rogoff, B., Mosier, C., Mystry, J. and Göncü, A. (1998) *Toddlers' Guided Participation with Caregivers in Cultural Activity*. London: Routledge.

Van Oers, B. (2010) 'Children's enculturation through play', in L. Brooker and S. Edwards (eds), *Engaging Play*. Maidenhead: Open University Press.

Wood, D. (1998) *How Children Think and Learn*. Oxford: Blackwell.

CHAPTER 9

The influence of learning environments

Chapter overview

This chapter considers how the nature of the materials offered to young children may be more likely to enable certain types of interaction, particularly playful interaction. The idea of 'affordance' is presented as a useful aid to our thinking when selecting the range of materials offered to children and the types of interaction that materials may support. Planning for and discussing playful engagement in activities with parents attending dual-focus groups can be helped by reflecting on what different activities afford children's experiences. A session with a high proportion of tactile abstract materials may afford plenty of opportunity for children engaged with control but it may afford few opportunities for adults to engage in negotiating the purpose, meaning and emotional aspects. This chapter includes a brief introduction to the theory of 'affordance ' which suggests that objects have a 'demand value' which exerts a particular pull towards certain types of activity. The nature and value of materials that are likely to engage adults and children playfully together is considered as a vehicle for nurturing social, emotional and cognitive development in unison.

Enabling environments

In England the phrase 'enabling environments' has become very widespread in the context of creating provision for young children (Department for Education, 2012). This phrase captures the idea of early education acknowledging the strengths of young children as pro-active learners and seeks to accord them greater control over their activity. The phrase 'enabling environment' has been adopted to promote the idea that children should be offered more control over their choices of activity and in their activity in order to develop autonomy and thinking.

Chapter 8 argued that we should be checking that we are enabling children to interact in a variety of ways with the adults in their environment. In the context of joint activities with parents it also highlighted two broad purposes for children's learning within groups. Sometimes we would like children to be independent so that they develop independence, confidence, sensory, coordination and control skills and there are also times when we want to emphasise more socially-orientated activity. The modes of interaction identified in Chapter 8 – controlling, monitoring and affirming, directing learning, sharing ideas and playing – fit with and reflect the shared purposes of adults and children which are negotiated and agreed between participants in the enactment of the activity. If we wish to facilitate opportunities for a range of learning within group situations, then careful thought should be given to the types of materials offered.

The idea of 'affordance' can be helpful in supporting reflection on the nature of the materials and the opportunities for interaction that they present. I was first introduced to the concept of affordances through two articles by Carr (2000, 2001) that explained how different materials offered up different possibilities to children's activities. Carr showed how the mechanics of a painted marble making patterns on papers placed in a box lid was a more transparent activity to pre-schoolers compared with a silk screen printing activity which required intense and quite directive adult supervision. Carr identified value in both activities but the roller-ball activity offered greater control opportunities to the child and for experimentation and child-to-child mentoring.

⚷ Key idea: affordances

Rogoff (1990) explains the attraction for those educationalists who subscribe to Vygotsky's (1978) view of social-cultural learning and Gibson's (1979) theory of affordances. Affordance theory offers an explanation of a cognitive base in the child's mind upon which cultural interactions might build. In essence, affordance theory suggests that, as with all other creatures, human senses have evolved to allow us to respond quickly to survive in our evolutionary niche. Our minds have evolved to be sensitive to particular messages from the environment as 'an event in which the animal seeks information relevant to functioning effectively in the environment and transforms itself to better fit its niche' (Rogoff, 1990: 31). Wertsch (1985) also points out the idea of affordance as being of interest to those who believe in social-cultural learning theories because it offers an explanation for how the individual interacts with the social and for how we might come to shared understandings.

Gibson (1979) showed how children are sensitive to the surfaces of materials, predicting whether they will be hard or soft, sticky or smooth. He argued that there are clear evolutionary advantages to being able to both predict where an object will be (in order to catch hold of it) and to anticipate how it needs to be handled. Apes, for example, need to be able to form effective judgements about the ability of branches to take their weight. So in the same way that we know children are paying close attention to faces to make sense of the faces, they are also paying close attention to the controllability of objects always from the point of view of how they might serve their purposes. 'The affordance of an object is what an infant begins by noticing. The meaning is observed, I think apprehended would be better here, before the substance and surface and colour and form' (Gibson, 1979: 134). Gibson (1979) points to the evolutionary advantages that accrue by perceptual receptors being sensitive and tuned to focus on size, style of movement, facial expressions, and to associate fight or flight instincts with these perceptions. These skills might then be further sharpened or moderated by social interactions.

In the 1930s Vygotsky was also seeking to acknowledge the ability of objects or situations to conjure a particular set of responses almost instantaneously in the mind. Like Gibson he also drew on Lewin (1935) and the Gestalt School's ideas who were also seeking to explain how humans came to perceive the world in similar ways. 'Many things attract the child to eating, others to climbing, to grasping, to manipulation, to sucking, to raging at them, etc. These environmental facts, we shall call them valences [Aufforderungcharaktere], determine the direction of the behaviour' (Lewin, 1935: 77). It is interesting to note that 'demand value' is also suggested in a note by the translator of Lewin's work as an alternative translation of Aufforderungcharaktere. This clearly resonates with the idea

(Continues)

(Continued)

of affordances as a perceptual force field triggering emotional, social and experiential responses to whole events not necessarily each constituent part of an event.

Del Rio and Alvarez (2007) point out that in exploring this new frontier, Vygotsky's (1978) key contribution was to highlight that humans have evolved by being able to mediate experience through the creation of tools to adapt to their environment: 'We might say that the adults lend the child, enslaved to his field in his passive attention, their active attention through this process of highlighting stimuli and capturing and guiding the child's gaze towards cultural affordances' (Del Rio et al., 2007: 287).

Neuroscience developments are also providing increasing evidence to support the view that patterns of action and purpose are at the forefront of the way we perceive the world. While magnetic resonance imaging cannot read peoples thoughts, it does show that images of particular types of objects instantly trigger certain patterns of activity in the brain which are categorised by eating and controlling (Sharot, 2012). Neuroscience studies show that consciousness is generated across the brain in the instant of experience and that senses, emotion and expectations are strong partners in forming the logical model of object (Greenfield, 2008).

Categories of affordance

Gibson (1979) identifies categories of affordance which offer some useful points for reflection when trying to identify the basic building blocks of joint attention and intersubjectivity between adults and children. The first of these relates to purposeful benefits to the individual: 'the affordances of the environment are what it offers the animal for good or ill' (Gibson, 1979: 127). Gibson goes on to note that these will be relative values depending on the size and nature of the animal.

The treasure baskets advocated by Goldschmied and Jackson (1993) that contain artefacts for very young children to handle, feel, shake, taste, stroke, tap would be an example of this. When young children engage with treasure baskets we see them identifying the benefits of the objects which are purposeful to them. Can they bite it? Can they get comfort or enjoyment from it? Exploratory creative activities with no clearly defined outcome, such as finger painting, mark-making or sensory play in water or sand may be more likely to facilitate individual play. When adults adopt monitoring and affirming modes, they create spaces for children to investigate and move towards independent self-managed activity. If practitioners wish to enable this, then the learning environment should offer activities which are open to children's interpretation and transparently sensory.

The second category of affordances that Gibson draws attention to relates to complex judgements around interactions with other creatures: 'What other animals afford above all, is a rich complex set of interactions, sexual, predatory, nurturing, fighting, playing, cooperating and communicating' (Gibson, 1979; 128). Dual-focused groups offer children new opportunities to engage with other children and adults beyond the home and family. This undoubtedly provokes emotional responses and adults are often monitoring and helping to control children's responses to sharing space and resources with other children.

In a social creature, perceptions need to be sensitive to attitudes, moods, subtle expressions and to an awareness of the motives of others competing for the same resources. Therefore being alongside others requires recognising shared meanings:

> Only when each child perceives the value of things for others as well as herself does she begin to be socialised ... What other persons afford is the whole realm of social significance for human beings. We pay closest attention to the optical and acoustic information that specifies what the person is, invites, threatens and does. (Gibson, 1979: 128)

In directed learning, practitioners and parents are drawn to lead children towards specific skills, meaning or knowledge. This is more likely to occur in activities with obvious opportunities for counting, naming colours or shape and may prompt adults to pursue these lines of teaching or questioning with children. Similarly, activities that require lots of help and guidance to make them work, or to achieve a particular image, for example to make a flower, are likely to prompt adults into more directive engagements.

Sometimes practitioners may see this form of interaction as problematic where it stifles the children's initiative or interests. It might also lead to frustrating interactions where the child is asked to do something beyond their zone of proximal development. Nevertheless it can be a mode that is frequently used and when it gels with children's interests and abilities it can be rewarding for both adult and child.

Shared learning activities in which children are more actively clarifying meaning with others are likely to be those which are more open ended. They are more often activities which also connect with previous sessions or interests so that children have enough experience to be able to take the activity forward. Simultaneously they provide adults with enough background knowledge to be able to help children make connections forwards and backwards in time. In these cases children actively seek to make sense of their experience and link it to the world of shared meaning.

The third category of affordance that Gibson notes relates to items not being perceived simply in their own right but in relation to how control might be applied to serve a purpose: 'Detached objects must be comparable in size to the animal under consideration if they are to afford behaviour. Nevertheless, those that are comparable, offer an astonishing variety of behaviours, especially to animals with hands. Objects can be manufactured and manipulated' (Gibson, 1979: 133).

The intensity of young children trying to master the control of objects and processes is apparent in many of the examples already presented in Chapters 6 and 7. The word 'play' is often used to describe those moments when a child is lost in concentration with scissors to cut tape or a paint roller to print images. In this sense play is rehearsal, exploration, practice and the blending of physical, emotional and intellectual control. Activities in which children become self-absorbed are precious, however we might also want to provoke play which involves others and enables children to explore ideas they would not reach on their own.

Aspects of affordance

In planning activities the pull of objects on children's thinking might draw them towards or away from particular intentions. So, for example, if a young child is more likely to 'see' a pen as something to suck on or chew rather than perceive it as a mark-making implement, offering more tactile finger-painting activities might be a more helpful starting point. Where adults and children are both converging on similar elements of experience then the interactions are more likely to be shared, sustained and reflexive.

In practice affordance theory can be particularly helpful in offering a simple framework for reflecting on the aspects of experience that form the meeting points for adults' and children's minds. If the idea of affordance is simply categorised into control, feeling, purpose and meaning it can help adults to think about tying their ideas to appropriate connecting points for engaging with children's thinking.

When these four types of affordance were used to categorise the examples of adult–child interaction presented in Chapter 8, they suggested different patterns of attention between the practitioners and parents. Each of the 63 episodes was coded in relation to the types of affordances foregrounded in the episode, either in terms of the child's focus of attention or by the joint attention of the adult and child. There were episodes with a single type of affordance and some with multiple types.

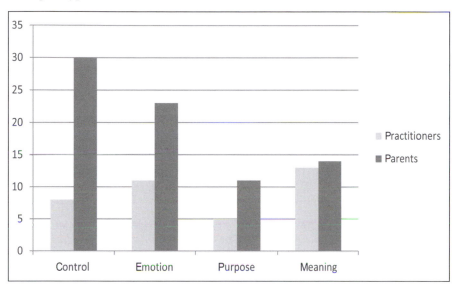

Figure 9.1   Comparing the frequency of affordance categories in episodes with adults present

Figure 9.1 suggests that in the episodes with practitioners present, meaning featured more frequently, whereas the episodes in which parents were present often involved control. This may be because the practitioners allowed meanings to come to the forefront in activities. It could also have been a result of them gravitating towards materials that offer opportunities to share meaning more consistently and frequently. These findings suggest that the environments in these particular parent and child groups presented activities where children could explore the control and feel of materials, but presented fewer opportunities to focus on the purpose and meaning of materials.

The following examples explore the potential role of affordance in shaping experiences. In the first example Farhad has rich opportunities for personal reflection on the sensory and control affordances of the water and objects. To some extent his older sister reveals the purpose of the funnel. However the activity remains very much on this sensory plane.

Farhad, 20 months, with Mum monitoring

Farhad returns to the water where Ejaz is already playing wearing a tall hat and pouring water from a small yoghurt bottle into a waterwheel. 'I'm in the water' says Ejaz to Farhad.

Farhad watches as Ejaz continues to pour water from a small cup to make the waterwheel spin around. He then hears a second waterwheel squeak as a work experience student pours water into it. Farhad pulls Ejaz's wheel closer to him to peer into the yellow funnel at the top and then uses a measuring jug to pour water in. He takes up the cup that Ejaz had been using and has a little sip of water and tips the rest into the funnel to make the wheel spin 'oy oy oy' he announces loudly to Ejaz as they both pour water onto the wheel. Farhad's elder sister arrives at the water tray and he looks and smiles broadly at her as she arrives. 'Oh oh' he says.

Farhad pours more water into the wheel with the measuring jug. 'Oo oo oo' he says and watches his sister pouring water out of a yogurt bottle into the water. He then begins to pour water on himself and his mum says, 'No Farhad' and watches her as she moves away. 'Oooo dad a' he says to his sister as she pours water into the funnel of the waterwheel. Farhad has noticed water dripping from the bottom of the cup he is pouring from and the work experience student shows Farhad how to hold the cup steady so that the water drips straight down out of the four holes into the bottom of the cup.

The following examples of interactions are contrasted with this first episode in order to illustrate the potential difference between a less and a more reflective exchange. In the next example, Farhad is initially offered the opportunity to connect animal figures with their names and the noises that they make. This foregrounds the potential of these figures to symbolise meanings that are shared between Farhad and his mother. Farhad is being prepared with the type of knowledge he will be expected to acquire but this is connected only weakly to themes which might engage and sustain the exchange.

Farhad, 20 months, with Mum

Mum starts laying some train track from a basket on the shelf, moving away from the base of the shelves. Farhad has picked up a yellow car and seems to be considering dropping the car on a smaller boy who is approaching. His mother catches the car as it drops and then tries to distract Farhad with a model giraffe from a basket.

'Giraffe,' she says.

He takes the giraffe and puts it down. She then says 'tiger', offering him a tiger. Farhad takes the tiger and shows it to the researcher who pretends to roar. Mum offers Farhad a tiger cub and says 'Tiger'.

Farhad says 'grrrr,' and shows the tiger to mum who offers him a horse. 'Horsey, horsey clip clop,' she says.

Farhad takes the horse and puts its mouth to the ground pretending it is feeding.

'Moo,' says mum giving Farhad a cow.

Farhad takes the cow and Martin asks if it is hungry like the horse.

'I bet it would like some grass too,' he suggests.

Farhad takes the cow and drops it carefully into the stable building of the farm. He takes a series of animals and repeats this action.

This example featuring Farhad contrasts with the Henry episode below where he is being asked to reflect on his feelings about the roller and the smell and texture of the paint. The connection of meaning to rich sensory and control experience seem to create a more resonant exchange, and this questioning seems to draw out the statement from Henry about mixing the paint. This fits in stylistically with a reflexive discussion in terms of an observation about the nature of the materials offered. Henry's mum also asks him to reflect on whether he likes using the roller. It would appear that Henry is already used to and comfortable with engaging in this type of discussion. Both Yasmeen, the practitioner, and Henry's mum offer a similar type of discourse that is able to prepare Henry very well for the type of questions he is likely to encounter in preschool and school.

Henry, 34 months, with practitioner Yasmeen

Yasmeen asks, and with Henry nodding, she squirts some of the washing up liquid on to the painting and some on his hand. 'There you are, wow.'

Henry looks carefully at the spongy roller that now has lots of tiny bubbles on it. 'What does it feel like?' she asks.

'It's blue and yellow,' replies Henry.

'Can you smell it?'

'I can smell it.'

'What does it smell like?'

[couldn't pick up Henry's answer]

'It smells of lemon,' says Yasmeen. 'Is it slippery when you touch it?'

'Blue and yellow make orange,' says Henry.

(Continues)

(Continued)

'Blue and yellow make orange,' says Yasmeen. 'Wow.'
Henry continues to use the roller and he looks over towards his mum who is looking after his younger sister.
'Look mummy look.'
'What are you doing?' asks mum.
Henry continues to roller sponge.
Mum picks up the blue paint and puts some more on to the paper. 'There, covered,' she says, 'Can I have a look at what you've done?' asks mum. 'Do you like painting with the roller?'
'Can you put some on?' asks Henry.
'That's very good,' says mum.

The above episodes help to illustrate that shared sustained thinking (SST) is different from simply extended joint activity, and the nature of interactive exchanges can frame the variety of connections that children are guided towards. The questions offered in the Henry example provide a structure, that if sustained, sets down a pattern of questioning and enquiry. The Farhad example connects object, language and sound but does not offer the same questioning and opinion valuing frameworks as the Henry example.

A pedagogy of activity, affordance and play

In the examples presented so far, the materials offered in the environments clearly appealed to the children's interests and have a level of transparency that enable the children to engage with them independently. The analysis of affordance can help to make visible the attention given by children and adults to sensory experience and gaining control over objects. The examples also illustrate that while children are often content to explore possibilities for control independently, meaning and purpose feature more prominently when the adults engage with the children. This of course is not surprising.

If some parents appeared to find playing in groups difficult it may have been that some of the materials absorbed children so completely that the adults' roles tended towards monitoring and affirming children's exploratory play. In cases where adults sought to guide children's attention in particular directions, there seemed to be success when it tallied in some way with the aspect of affordances recognised by the children.

The more playful exchanges between adults and children tended to give rise to more extended reflections and the objects had greater potential for shared meaning. One form of play was simply to share in children's experiences. This is illustrated in the following example of a play activity that followed the previous week's session in which parents and children had covered a balloon with paper mache and covered the hardened structure with glue and glitter. The play had a more exploratory orientation rather than a game format.

Abas, 24 months, with practitioner Julie and child Jane

Abas moves from the home corner area to stand at the large tray of gold glitter where Julie is already sitting talking with Jane. Mum remains behind watching from the other side of the room. Abas picks up handfuls of the gold glitter from the tray and holds them up.

'Are you squeezing them?' asks Julie. He allows the glitter to fall out of his hand. He looks up at two parents standing nearby and watches them talking as he feels the glitter in the tray with his fingers. He presses both palms into the glitter and studies each one before clapping his hands together hard and watching the glitter spray off in both directions. He repeats this touching then clapping several times. He sprinkles the glitter from one hand onto the other.

'Are you sprinkling it from hand to hand?' asks Julie.

Abas suddenly looks towards his mother. 'Mummy,' he calls.

'I'm just here', she reassures him from the home corner area. He goes over to her and brings her back to the glitter tray and he resumes pouring the glitter.

'Sparkles,' says Julie. Abas repeats the touching and clapping.

'This is why we come here so we don't have this mess at home' says mum.

Abas shows a palm full of glitter to Julie who says 'ready' as she indicates that she is going to blow the glitter. They blow together, Abas laughs out loud and the others also laugh. They repeat this.

Abas moves off towards the washroom with his mum. They return shortly and mum again remains on the other side of the room while Abas returns to the glitter to continue blowing the glitter gently from his hands. Another child has placed a large baby doll in the tray and Abas sprinkles glitter onto its forehead. He blows a palm full of glitter over the doll.

'That was a great big puff of wind,' says Julie as Abas looks to her and laughs out loud again. He heads back over to his mum and draws her with him towards the bathroom.

'He just likes to use the hand-dryer' she explains 'that is all it is.'

Abas soon returns to the glitter tray. He holds the baby by the waist and dips its feet gently in the glitter. He puts the doll down and holds another handful of glitter towards Julie. 'Do you want to put it on my hand?'

(Continues)

(Continued)

He sprinkles the glitter onto Julie's hand.

'Oh wow!' she says.

Abas tentatively licks the glitter. 'It doesn't taste nice' says Julie.

Abas tries to head for the bathroom a third time and mum catches him by the waist and turns him round saying that he doesn't need to wash his hands until he is finished. He returns to the glitter tray and he holds up another handful of glitter for Julie to blow which she does. Abas then moves towards the toilets again where he uses the hand-dryer to blow the glitter of his hands. He washes his hands and then blows them dry, supported by his mother. He then skips back from the bathroom to the glitter tray.

Here the materials seem to motivate Abas to develop control and sensory enjoyment. Julie recognises and shares this pleasure in parallel to Abas. She introduces blowing to the activity which develops both the control and sensory affordances of the materials and begins to form the basis of signifiers for more figurative interactions. 'That was a great big puff of wind' introduces a more social semantic aspect to the interaction: it is a simple and transparent metaphor and it is a step towards substituting one thing for another that will move play into richer symbolic territory (Pramling and Pramling-Samuelsson, 2009). It begins to show us how play provides the opportunity to gain insight into how others perceive the world. This leads us back to Vygotsky's (1978) interest in the power of objects and the power of play to transform a stick into a 'horse'.

The trick to engaging in playing with meaning is to spot how the affordances children are interested in might connect to more imaginative situations. Adults are seeking words or actions that may conjure up alternative schema. These should resonate with present and past patterns and connect experience to new possibilities in children's minds potentially inspiring new activities and dialogue.

It is possible that some parents might benefit from reassurance that even young children's schemas can relate to complex systems of activity as well as basic patterns of movement. The affordance that an object invokes regulates its potential for activity and changing the focus of activity may inform the development of the use of the object. If the objects in early education environments only focus on creative activities, then the range of activity may be limited to sensory and control experiences.

In the last part of this chapter I explore the age appropriateness of pretend play and the potential for this type of play to generate more dialogic exchanges. In the final example Maisy is inside a large playhouse in the middle of the outdoor play area. There is a window, a table and benches downstairs as well as stairs to an upper floor with a bed. There is also a cupboard with cooking toys.

Maisy, 21 months, with practitioner Mary and mother Helen

Maisy goes back into the house and asks Mary and her mum to return inside.

'I'm going up stairs, I'm going to find a bed', she announces and stamps up the steps and on to the upper floor.

'Is that a giant up there?' Mary asks, 'it sounded like a giant.'

She comes back down the stairs smiling and picks up the car.

'Is that the giant's toy?' asks Mary.

'I'm going to put it in the oven', she says.

Mary asks if she is going to cook it for the giant to eat.

Maisy opens the top half of the stable door and says hello to her mum who replies. 'Shut it, please shut it,' she asks her mum who is outside. 'Squish, squish,' she says pushing it closed. She goes back up the steps and three other children come in and wave to Maisy. Maisy picks up a wooden box she has found up the stairs and picks it up. 'Is it too heavy?' asks Mary.

'Look, a box,' she says and starts to bring it down the stairs.

'What's in the box?' asks Mary.

'Golden coins,' she answers smiling.

['that's the pirate influence,' says her mum, explaining that Maisy has a 5-year-old brother and 9-year-old sister whom she plays with a lot.]

Maisy has moved outside again and is looking at the bread crates. 'Are you going along there?' asks her mum. Maisy does so once and then climbs on to a tricycle. 'I find you,' she says to Mary as she returns to the front of the house.

'Shall we hide the giant's treasure?' suggests Mary.

Maisy places the box on the bench beside the side of the playhouse. Mary pretends to look for it in a couple of places and then finds it on the bench. 'Ah, there it is, I found it.' She then hides the box in some tyres next to the playhouse and Maisy runs off to three corners of the play area looking for it. Mary offers a clue. 'Look over here,' she suggests. This activity is repeated several times with Maisy increasingly using words to regulate the play. 'It's in the wheels,' 'Have you found it yet?,' 'It's in the sand,' 'Me hide it again,' 'Me hide it in the sand,' frequently giving away the location of the box in requesting Mary to find it again.

'I'll hide it in the wheel,' she says.

The playhouse and its contents cry out to be used for pretend play because they are obviously representations of human activity. The environment is already heavily laden with meanings, the objects suggest actions, roles and storylines to Maisy that she is familiar with. The amount of language elicited in this context also contrasted sharply to the indoor environment where the materials mostly appeared to afford Maisy opportunities to develop control over materials. The larger scale as well as the more culturally symbolic artefacts seemed to trigger more language-laden responses for Maisy. The vocabulary of everyday objects is familiar and allow greater scope for play and manipulation of meaning than the more experiential and craft orientated activities.

In this example language adds layers of meaning to the objects, connecting them to stories across time and promoting anticipation of actions between the participants. Playing together is predicated upon the establishment of shared agreements regarding goals, rules and roles. It is therefore rich in dialogic exchange and the potential for guiding the use of physical and abstract tools.

In dual-focused settings it is helpful for practitioners to help parents get to know the language they use for different materials offered in sessions. Practitioners may find it helpful to model a range of modes and mention to parents what they were trying to do in different situations. The latest practices being employed at Pen Green (Haywood, 2013), where video is used to promote dialogue about practitioner styles of interaction, may offer profitable methods for practitioner and perhaps parental development.

Practitioners may also find it helpful to think about what the range of materials in a session might offer to children. A session with a high proportion of tactile abstract materials may afford plenty of opportunity for children engaged with control but it may afford few opportunities for adults to engage in negotiating the purpose, meaning and emotional aspects. These are strengths of role play that become so significant in the pre-school 3–5 age range because it offers the opportunity for children to explore these aspects in great depth and subtlety.

Authors such as Rogers (2010), Van Oers (2010) and Edmiston and Taylor (2010) advocate the value of adults supporting the play process, particularly in role play, without controlling the play agenda to such an extent that the benefits of play are lost. They highlight that the process of adults 'lending ideas' through language and action seems to offer a clearer pathway towards more reflective forms of thinking: 'I suggest that an alternative view of play pedagogy might be as a negotiated "space", both physical and conceptual, for children and teachers to explore identities and desires, and evaluate questions of voice and power in the classroom' (Rogers, 2010: 163).

The more abstracted, negotiated social meanings involved in pretend play should be compared to the more 'directed learning' and 'monitoring/supporting' modes afforded by materials that demand control and exploration so that a balance of activities can be offered in enabling environments. I would suggest that if we consider it appropriate to guide children towards educational interactions in school and preschool, then it should also be appropriate for adults to support children towards the pretend play skills that form a key element of the pre-school experience.

〰️ **Reflective activities: affordances**

This chapter has focused on how different activities and artefacts lend themselves to different facets of exploration and interaction. Identify an activity within a setting and reflect on the type of experiences you anticipate it will afford to children and parents. Carry out an observation of the activity and try to reflect on what opportunities for reflection on control, purpose, emotion and meaning emerge during the activity and who initiates these. Discuss with the families what types of responses they had to the materials and what they were inspired to talk about. Reflect with them on what adaptations to the activity might extend the activity in a new direction.

References 📖

Carr, M. (2001) 'Emerging learning narratives', in G. Wells and G. Claxton (eds), *Learning for Life in the 21st Century*. London: Blackwell.

Carr, M. (2000) 'Technological affordance, social practice and learning narratives in an early childhood setting', *International Journal of Technology and Design Education*, 10: 61–79.

Del Rio, P. and Alvarez, A. (2007) 'Inside and outside the zone of proximal development', in H. Daniels, M. Cole and J.V. Wertsch (eds), *The Cambridge Companion to Vygotsky*. New York: Cambridge University Press.

Department for Education (DfE) (2012) *Framework for the Early Years Foundation Stage: Setting the Standards for Learning, Development and Care for Children from Birth*. London: Department for Education.

Edmiston, B. and Taylor, T. (2010) 'Using power on the playground', in L. Brooker and S. Edwards (eds), *Engaging Play*. Maidenhead: Open University Press.

Gibson, J. (1979) *The Ecological Approach to Visual Perception*. Boston, MA: Houghton Miflin Company.

Goldschmied, E. and Jackson, S. (1993) *People Under Three: Young Children in Day Care*. London: Routledge.

Greenfield, S.A. (2008) *I.D. The Quest for Identity in the 21st Century*. London: Sceptre.

Haywood, K. (2013) 'Being in relation', symposium at the 23rd EECERA conference, Tallinn University, Tallinn, Estonia, 28–31 August.

Lewin, K. (1935) *A Dynamic Theory of Personality*. New York: McGraw-Hill.

Pramling, N. and Pramling-Samuelsson, I. (2009) 'The prosaics of figurative language in preschool: some observations and suggestions for research', *Early Child Development and Care*, 179(3): 329–38.

Rogers, S. (2010) 'Powerful pedagogies and playful resistance', in L. Brooker and S. Edwards (eds), *Engaging Play*. Maidenhead: Open University Press.

Rogoff, B. (1990) *Apprenticeship Thinking in the Social Context*. New York: Open University Press.

Sharot, T. (2012) *Science Club: Reproduction*, BBC 2 Television, viewed 23 December.

Van Oers, B. (2010) 'Children's enculturation through play', in L. Brooker and S. Edwards (eds), *Engaging Play*. Maidenhead: Open University Press.

Vygotsky, L.S. (1978) *Mind and Society*. Cambridge, MA: Harvard University Press.

Wertsch, J.V. (1985) *Vygotsky and the Social Formation of Mind*. Cambridge, MA: Harvard University Press.

CONCLUDING CHAPTER

CHAPTER 10

Developing transitional capital

Chapter overview

A number of authors argue that transitions should not be viewed as problematic stages to be smoothed over and moved through quickly, but rather as life events that can be approached and embraced as important learning opportunities (Brooker, 2008; Dunlop and Fabian, 2007). During our own research there were many times when adults viewed joint parent and child activities as ways in which to prepare children for the next step in their education. That is, there was a focus on teaching children how to move away from parents and home and towards 'teachers' and schools, and this reflects the findings reported by Brooker (2008) and Dunlop and Fabian (2007). In the context of transitions, we argue that dual-focused groups should be valued in their own right as an important venue for nurturing both parents and children. This final chapter demonstrates how these types of early years' settings offer rich opportunities to develop important skills and confidence to cope with life transitions more generally, both for children and their parents. We conclude by emphasising the importance of celebrating transitions as routes by which the establishment of trusting relationships and patterns of learning can be nurtured. We show that joint activities involving children, parents and practitioners in dual-focused groups can be conceptualised as robust opportunities to develop transitional capital (Brooker, 2008; Dunlop and Fabian, 2007).

Introduction

Brooker (2008) emphasises the importance of adults acting as a bridge between the cultures of belief and practice in the home and in early childhood education: 'Taking a positive rather than negative view of transitions requires a shift in perspective from "readiness", though it depends similarly on a two-pronged focus for action; working with schools and settings and working with children' (Brooker, 2008: 142). Group activities such as those discussed in this book are uniquely placed to create a joint space for bridge-building by bringing children, practitioners and parents together. However, in order to recognise the potential to develop children's transition skills, Brooker (2008: 141) argues that practitioners should address two areas: 'mediating the discontinuities between cultures' and supporting the 'development of resources for change'. Clearly dual-focused groups offer important spaces for parents, children and practitioners to gain insights into each others' purposes, language and thinking as they negotiate new contexts beyond home.

As personal resources for change, Brooker (2008) identifies five areas for supporting children's skills in transitioning: resilience, resourcefulness, reciprocity, reflection and rights. These areas relate to helping children take stock of their emotional intelligence, adaptability, and awareness of others and the rules that apply to themselves and others in a new context. In this final chapter we explore these areas in more detail shortly, however, it is important to note that parent and child groups enable children to experience these areas of support with their parents who inhabit both cultural spaces with them. Further, Dunlop draws on Bourdieu's (1997) analysis of culture to analyse the value of paying attention to the value of transitions:

> Here, the emphasis is placed on culture, the importance of habitus and different forms of capital, support the argument that we may carry forward factors influencing our lives in a variety of ways. If little capital accrues to the child at the first transition; subsequently, there may be less to draw on (Dunlop and Fabian, 2007: 158).

🔑 Key idea: Bourdieu and social capital

Bourdieu (1997) argues that the process of education is bound up with the transmission of cultural capital. Cultural capital relates to the knowledge we have about how to relate to the world and our ability to participate in activities within different cultural groupings. Bourdieu uses the term 'habitus' to describe the amalgam of habits, attitudes, and behaviours that individuals acquire and present to others as their identity. Three forms of cultural capital are identified by Bourdieu:

- embodied cultural capital which relates to the knowledge and skills embodied in a person and habitus of that individual;
- objectified cultural capital such as books and artefacts; and
- the institutionalised grouping of people by the processes of their education and marked by qualifications.

In other words the skills that individuals possess in order to participate in cultural contexts gives them access to resources. The more skilled they are in engaging with those particular contexts, the more able they are to gain from participation in them. Some contexts yield more resources than others and some, such as education, are often tightly controlled by codes which legitimate knowledge, language and behaviour.

Bourdieu (1997) argues that while the process of education seems to offer families a route to increased cultural capital which might then be converted into social and economic capital, its propensity to reproduce existing societal stratifications is concealed. Often teachers and schools tend to confer more upon children who behave appropriately and open up more to children with certain interests and knowledge. 'More precisely cultural capital, whose diffuse, continuous transmission within the family escapes observation and control (so that the education system seems to award its honours solely on natural qualities)' (Bourdieu, 1997: 55).

We argue that dual-focused groups can potentially make educational discourses and expectations more visible to parents who can, in turn and over time, help mediate these discourses to their children.

Recommended further reading

Dunlop, A. and Fabian, H. (2007) *Informing Transitions in the Early Years.* Maidenhead: Open University Press.

Brooker (2008) identified that in early transitions children are often seen as being prepared for school. This happens through the introduction of state legitimised cultural capital relating to the behaviours and knowledge that are endorsed through the introduction to artefacts and materials endorsed as valuable by the state and required by schools. This danger can also be present in dual-focused groups in the attention given to preparing children for school tasks. In order to mediate this risk, practitioners should mindfully focus and draw attention to well-being, skills and attitudes in the present. They can foreground and support the building of social and cultural capital related to personal confidence and dealing with others as skills which will benefit children in many contexts which include but are not limited to school.

In this book we have chosen to highlight three interconnected aspects of children's experience:

- managing emotional intelligence;
- adapting to new rules and cultures; and
- learning to form new relationships.

These three aspects intersect with each other and with the five competencies identified by Brooker (2008): resilience, resourcefulness, reciprocity, reflection and rights. By enabling joint activity between parents, children and practitioners in dual-focused early years' settings and encouraging support in these five areas, we are able to help develop children's abilities for subsequent transitions. For example, having made one transition, a child's resilience to change may be enhanced so that she or he may be able to assume more responsibility during future transitions. She or he will have a greater range of experience and strategies to draw upon, aligned with a better understanding of the requirement to adjust to other people's needs and to fit in with group practices. Further, by talking about these points and drawing attention to features that support transition, parents and practitioners are able to scaffold children's abilities to reflect on different elements of social contexts, the rules of behaviour, communication, learning and participation. In this way children are given the opportunity to learn about how they might expect to be treated in a particular context, that is, how much control they might have over their actions, how much interference there might be from others or how long they might have to sit and wait. Significantly, in dual-focused groups, parents are able to mediate the differences between home and group culture which may substantially support the children's learning and confidence. This mediation is illustrated from this quote from a school principal in Jackson's (2010) research.

Case study

How to talk, to make friends, to share, how to be in a group. Even just coming in and saying 'bye mum' – those sort of social skills so they are not clingy and scared, it's a comfort thing. There has been a big improvement in that; you can certainly notice that after playgroup interaction … because they've had to interact with others and they've had to do it in an environment where … the mere fact that it is attached to the school is brilliant because they've had to do it in an environment where coming to school is normal … I think it's fantastic and also they've had to share and play and talk and discuss in an environment that isn't home … it's totally a new area and they've had to become comfortable there and they've done it with mum or dad's support, so it's non-threatening … (School Principal)

Managing emotional intelligence

There are a number of strategies that parents can adopt to support their children's developing emotional intelligence in new contexts. They can model confidence in entering the new environment, help children recognise features which are similar to home and objects that are exciting and easy to master. Similarly, parents can also help children manage their frustration when learning to engage with new objects and systems.

In subsequent educational transitions children may experience relatively little autonomy when entering the new culture and often they will spend limited, if any, time in the environment with their parents. In contrast, parent and child groups enable children to manage these processes within more traditional patterns of attachment which enable support and decrease occurrences that are potentially emotionally over-whelming. Parents can see what aspects of the new environment might be challenging and help children negotiate issues related to other children competing for resources, approaching new adults or complying with group time schedules.

In terms of developing transitional capital a link can also be made here to the concepts of secure base and 'letting go' behaviours and repertoires of practice (Rogoff et al., 2007) described in Chapter 6. It should also be remembered that for some parent-and-child dyads this may be their first opportunity to manage mutually supportive relationships beyond the immediate family. This is illustrated in the following quotes from Jackson's (2010) research.

Case study

I just think in D's case, playgroup's actually a very good bridge for him between being at home with us full time, and going to preschool, because he's got issues of security, and so he, probably more than many children, needs that opportunity to find his own – to move away from me in his own time, rather than just suddenly be thrown into preschool for five or six hours a day … because when we first got D [adopted child], he would just follow me around the house all the time, and would just be talking to me all the time. And so he obviously needed to be close to me all the time. And even at playgroup he didn't really move away much. But now he'll go and play on his own. So it's obviously built that for him. (Parent)

One thing I've found with my son is he's always been a really clingy child … so when he was young, that was really hard for me. But actually having come to playgroup, he's obviously met children here at playgroup that ended up at the same preschool, so starting preschool wasn't actually as hard as I thought, because there were some children at preschool that he'd known from playgroup, which was good for him. (Parent)

The Australian research undertaken on the supported playgroup model (Jackson, 2010) also alerts us to the significant role that these types of groups can play in children's transitions to new settings such as formal childcare or school. Children's responsiveness and attachment to adults other than their parents is fostered in these groups, and attachment theory again provides us with a framework to explain the importance of environments such as these in children's transitions.

Research undertaken in Western cultures, such as Australia, suggests that infants form hierarchies of attachment, with mothers generally being the primary attachment figure (Sims and Hutchins, 1999). Once secure attachment is formed with the primary figure, children are more likely to respond positively to other adults and go on to develop further attachment relationships with significant others, such as caregivers (Jordan and Sketchley, 2009; Reebye et al., 2009; Sims and Hutchins, 1999). Moreover, children's interactional patterns with their parents shape their expectations of how others will respond. Ideally, through secure attachment relationships with their primary carers, children develop 'working models' (Bretherton, 1992) or 'transition capital' (Brooker, 2008; Dunlop and Fabian, 2007) for other responsive and accessible relationships. For younger children in particular, having a parent with them means that they have that secure and comfortable base from which to explore the new setting, meaning that for some children they are more prepared for the sometimes deeply unsettling experience of being left alone in an educare setting.

Learning to recognise new rules and cultures

The parent accompanying a child to a dual-focus group can highlight and explain how the new rules in this space differ to those in the home, they can anticipate when their child will behave differently and act to reduce conflict, emphasise rights, show how to clarify rules by asking others and show how to clarify rules by watching what others do. We have looked in detail at the ways in which adults support children in the context of parent-and-child groups and at the variations in attitudes and expectations that different approaches to engaging with this early education environment might create. We have considered how parents take great care to help children share space and resources with other children who are equally uncertain about how to behave.

In Chapter 8 we examined how practitioners in supported playgroups might help to extend participants' awareness of the rules and roles possible in repertoires of practice related to play in an educare context. There is widespread consensus the play offers a potentially liberating and creative learning opportunity that children find particularly engaging, but the ground rules and roles within parent and toddler groups need to be considered carefully to achieve this.

Sociocultural theories suggests that play emerges from the social cultural context and not just from within the child (Bröström, 1999; Hakkarainen, 1999). Play is a complex and varied mode of social engagement that can be learned and developed. It is not something to be taken for granted. Those children with few or no siblings and in age-stratified nursery groups may find it helpful for adults to do more to initiate children into playfulness, compensating for a role which might in other social contexts be left more to other children. This process is not helped by the associations culturally and historically embedded in the word 'play', which serve to diminish its value and discourage adults' engagement in play.

Practitioners might find the labels for the modes of interaction developed in Part 2 helpful in enabling children to adopt both individual and collaborative modes of exploration and play that facilitate a wider range of learning opportunities. There may also be substantial benefits for some children if they are encouraged and enabled to engage with their parents through new modes of playful engagement in other contexts beyond the parent and toddler group. In contrast to pre-school-age children, 2-year-olds are far less likely to engage directly with others in this age group.

For play to be developed and sustained between two individuals, it requires the dialogic agreement of rules and purposes for each to maintain the participation of the other. It is suggested that playing is a valuable interactive mode in its own right and continues to be so in later life for those who learn to nurture and perfect it. An increase in the proportion of playful adult participation (Siraj-Blatchford, 2004) might be helpful not only in stretching children's thinking but in promoting open interactive relationships between children and adults.

Learning how to approach new people and develop relationships

Forming new relationships is an ongoing challenge to all of us and it requires complex social judgments about body language, expectations, joint interests and attention. This is an intricate synthesis of social, emotional and cognitive intelligence. Children will acquire social skills, strategies and confidence by engaging in groups with new contacts and interacting alongside and with others, mediated by communities of practice.

Transitioning together in environments which parents find supportive also helps to reduce parental anxiety and optimise the potential for the development of caring, friendly relationships between parents and facilitators (Jackson, 2010). In these ways, children are able to observe their parents' interactions with these other adults and are likely to infer that these people are safe people to interact with themselves. Through the process known as social referencing (Hutchins and Sims, 1999; Sims and Hutchins, 1999), supported playgroups and groups like them appear to create environments in which children positively reference their own behaviour to that of their parents and build trusting relationships over time with adults other than their parents, particularly facilitators.

The benefits of dual-focused groups in the development of relationships that support children's transition to school are also highlighted in research conducted by Jackson and Woodrow (2008). This research investigated multiple stakeholder perspectives on a project in western Sydney that ran 'Starting School' supported playgroups in schools for children in the year prior to them starting formal schooling. The groups were facilitated by early childhood teachers and the approach differed from more typical short-term transition or orientation programmes in that children and families participated together for up to 16 weeks during terms 3 and 4 prior to school commencement.

The collaborative nature of the model and the importance of developing strategies that enabled parents and children to engage in a transition process together emerged as significant findings in the research. As one of the research participants observed, 'When the child starts school, the family starts school'.

The research highlighted the strength of this type of dual-focused service which used a family-focused, relational approach to facilitate sustained relationships over an extended period. Importantly, the research identified distinctive characteristics that also align with the ideas presented so far in this chapter. In particular the groups:

- Were family focused. The model catered for parents and children together and therefore promoted the transition of the family to school rather than just the child.
- Sustained participation. The model fostered participation by families over a sustained period of time and this was what promoted the development of substantive relationships – unlike many programmes nationally and internationally that are established in the last few weeks prior to school commencement and are more focused on the child than the family.
- Informed decision-making. Parents had the opportunity to observe their children interacting in an educational environment with other children and adults, often for the first time. This informed their decisions about interactions and support in the environment and

whether or not they wanted their children to commence school the following year.

- Were relational. The model was relationship focused ᵃther than skill focused.
- Addressed family needs. The model used a universal format that also allowed targeted strategies to be embedded to meet individual needs.

We can see again that groups that invite the participation of parents and children together offer opportunities to both for sharing and learning. Parents and practitioners can also encourage independence by affirming children in these modes of engagement thus preparing them to engage with learning in the wider world. In this way children are encouraged to actively make meaning through interacting with people, objects and activities.

Developing practice

In a context where practitioners are expected to engage with parents, there is renewed emphasis on the importance of reflexive practice. Practitioners need to be even more aware of what they are doing and why they are doing it, and to be conscious of how they convey those messages to others. The clear tensions between the objectives of independence and improved interaction are something that would be useful to include in the framing of groups. To acknowledge the value of parents' perspectives in promoting independence might reduce tension within groups between leaders and participants, promoting increased levels of participation. Both the English and Australian case studies presented in this book suggest that if groups become too formal then some parents are likely to find that programmes are mismatched to their needs, which is why the Pen Green approach of modelling, discussion and shared research with families is so appealing (Whalley and the Pen Green Team, 2007).

Using research as demonstrated by Pen Green (Whalley and the Pen Green Team, 2007) can create a more flexible cultural space that focuses on constructing detailed meanings of events so practitioners' and parents' can exchange views more equally. Explicit modelling and discussion of styles by practitioners can help some parents broaden the range of interactive modes that they employ with their children. In our experience, practitioners, whatever their qualification, will always benefit from more opportunities to reflect on ways to develop the use of research with parents.

Campaigning to extend opportunities for dual-focus groups

We have shown how there has been a rapidly increasing level of professional interest and participation in activities with parents supported by the longitudinal findings from several countries (Schweinhart et al., 2005; Sylva et al., 2010; Wylie and Thompson, 2003) regarding the lasting benefits of pre-school. Many current government policies continue to favour increasing the provision of institutional pre-school places for children aged 2 and younger. However, in cases where these policies are specifically targeting 'disadvantaged' families without engaging parents, it would appear that there is a dual danger of presenting a deficit view of parents' skills and missing the opportunity for joint participation groups. Such policies may fail to acknowledge the significance of the home-learning environment in underpinning the effects of educational provision unless educare settings are able to create opportunities within their provision for families.

In addition, while the importance of parents has been registered by policy-makers, initiatives promoting activities with parents are still far less visible in comparison to pre-school provision and more might be done to promote the benefits of these groups to parents. The issue of reducing the clash in cultures between the language of the learner and school has long been identified and, yet, structures for bridging the gap between home and educational contexts have been slow to emerge (Bruner, 2006). The development and take up of joint play sessions may be a significant but relatively small step towards something that has the potential to improve understanding between home and school at a point when the gap between the two is not too wide. Dual-focus groups offer an opportunity to make the more elaborated codes of education more visible (Bernstein, 2003) to both parents and children. Parent and toddler groups could become part of the universal structure of education rather than an early intervention.

Potentially inhibiting factors to the take-up of dual-focused sessions include affordability, not in terms of the cost but in terms of the time taken out from employment and earning. Similarly the framing of sessions around parenting carries the danger of alienating parents sensitive to the inference that they are 'in deficit' (Parents as Partners in Early Learning, 2007). Further, if sessions are too educationally orientated some parents and children may experience negatively the pressure to behave and conform in particular ways causing them to opt out.

Parents greatly appreciate the opportunity for adult contact during days that can be dominated by family roles, so the opportunity for parents to talk freely with each other is a factor that requires consideration. There is plenty of evidence that points towards the long-term benefits of activities that involve parents, but there are few evaluations of specific models beyond prescribed parenting courses. There is a need for further research on how a range of different provisions might suit different parents. The promotion of social play spaces for parents and children offering a range of sessions has the potential to promote parents as active agents in children's participation in informal and more educational activities. Parents are willing to take this role and state policies should be careful not to disconnect parents from education at such an early stage.

The enhancement of flexible parental leave enabling women and men to take time during the week to spend with their children would genuinely acknowledge them as valued first educators. The provision of spaces for parents and children to be together at weekends would also facilitate wider participation in such activity. There are an increasing number of sessions for fathers and children offered in children's centres and other similar services in the UK and Australia. Simply making the early education environment available to both children and parents of both sexes might create a social space as popular with parents as parks, more popular on cold wet winter days. It is often argued that the cost of such services are likely to be prohibitive, and more research is needed with regard to the potential cost benefits of such developments with differing levels of professional participation. The personal cost to children who find accessing education challenging is already clear; the difficulties of promoting access to stigmatised targeted services are equally apparent. The promotion of universal services with targeted support for parents requires commitment but is not impossibly costly; provision in the form of school environments already exists along with the concept of extended schools. It is the instigation of play and learning coordinators that represents the additional expense and under-researched element.

In researching this topic and attending international conferences, we have found that there is parallel development occurring across industrialised nations resulting in increased professionally facilitated service provision for parents and children. There is also increasing interest in some of the rapidly industrialising nations. Simultaneously, there is a great deal of uncertainty and reflection taking place with regard to the role and relationship between parents/carers and professional educators. Early years professionals have strived and succeeded in establishing early childhood education principles distinct to those of school arguing that children's learning is different in focus and process in this phase. As services expand there is a pressing need to review provision for the under 3s, to consider how their learning might best be supported with the resources available to us, and the inclusion of parents should be central to this. Austerity budgets present a real threat to dual-focus groups. Recent government policy in England (DfE, 2013) has resulted in funding for children's centres focusing on a 'core offer' of priority early education places and targeted interventions, particularly on health education. Outreach services, of which parent and toddler groups may be considered a part, are under pressure from restrictions to local government expenditure. While early education places are increasing, there is a suggestion that outreach work with under 3s should be embedded in the family support provided by health visitors. There is danger that such a shift could reduce pedagogical input into these important family learning opportunities.

Dual-focus groups offer a very rich opportunity to support transition from the home learning environment to the educational learning environment on a much wider scale than has previously existed. Groups such as the ones presented in this book offer opportunities to develop the 'transitional capital' of both parents and children. They also afford parents environments in which to learn some of the vocabulary and attitudes of the professionals that could help them relate to teachers in later transitions. Further, children have the opportunity to see how adults establish new relationships in an institutional context and to be guided in establishing friendships with others. This being said, it would seem that there is an imperative for further research that identifies the different models of dual-focused service provision and the extent to which they facilitate ongoing family engagement. It is also critical to know what learning parents and children transfer to the home-learning environment as a result of participation.

While governments around the world are evincing an interest in developing the parents' role in education, and in a time of increasing financial pressure, it is essential that effective models of practice are documented and shared. If we are not able to develop and document these models quickly, the chance to expand towards a universal offer with regard to the provision of such services will pass. The early years sector needs to engage with parents' power, which through online social media groups is increasingly visible in politics, to lobby for approaches that are far more inclusive of parents.

〰️ **Reflective activities: learning from transitions**

Reflect on the last time you started in a new job or training course. Create a mind map of the skill sets and attitudes that helped you adapt. Identify how you would like to prepare yourself further for future transitions that you might make.

If you could have someone with you as you make a transition into a new context who would it be and why? This could be someone you know directly or someone famous. Share your thoughts with a colleague.

References

Bernstein, B. (2003) *Class, Codes and Control: Volume IV the Structuring of Pedagogic Discourse*. Abingdon: Routledge.

Bourdieu, P. (1997) 'The forms of capital.', in A.H. Halsey, H. Lauder, P. Brown and A. Stuart Wells (eds), *Education; Culture, Economy and Society*. Oxford: Oxford University Press. pp. 46–58.

Bretherton, I. (1992) 'The origins of attachment theory: John Bowlby and Mary Ainsworth', *Developmental Psychology*, 28(5): 759–75.

Brooker, L. (2008) *Supporting Transitions in the Early Years*. Maidenhead: Open University Press.

Bröström, S. (1999) 'Drama games with 6-year-old children: possibilities and limitations', in Y. Engeström, R. Miettinen and R.J. Punamaki (eds), *Perspectives on Activity Theory*. New York: Cambridge University Press.

Bruner, J. (2006) 'Poverty and childhood', in J. Bruner (ed), *In Search of Pedagogy*. Abingdon: Routledge. pp. 176–97.

Department for Education (DfE) (2013) *Improving the Quality and Range of Education and Childcare from Birth to 5 Years*, accessed 12 October 2013 at: www.gov.uk/government/policies/improving-the-quality-and-range-of-education-and-childcare-from-birth-to-5-years.

Dunlop, A. and Fabian, H. (2007) *Informing Transitions in the Early Years*. Maidenhead: Open University Press.

Hakkarainen, P. (1999) *Play and Motivation*. Cambridge: Cambridge University Press.

Hutchins, T. and Sims, M. (1999) *In Search of Relationships: An Ecological Approach to Planning for Infants and Toddlers*. Sydney: Prentice Hall.

Jackson, D. (2010) 'A place to "be": the role of supported playgroups in creating responsive, social spaces for parent and child wellbeing', unpublished doctoral thesis, University of Western Sydney.

Jackson, D. and Woodrow, C. (2008) 'Connections for learning: the role of supported playgroups in supporting transition to school', paper presented European Early Childhood Education Research Association conference, September.

Jordan, B. and Sketchley, R. (2009) 'A stitch in time saves nine: preventing and responding to the abuse and neglect of infants', *Child Abuse Prevention Issues*, 30, accessed 2 August 2009 at: www.aifs.gov.au/nch/pubs/issues/issues30/issues30.html

Parents as Partners in Early Learning (2007) *Parental Involvement – a Snapshot of Policy and Practice*. London: DCSF.

Reebye, P.N., Ross, S.E. and Jamieson, M.A. (2009) 'A literature review of child–parent/caregiver attachment theory and cross-cultural practices influencing attachment', accessed 1 September 2009 at: www.attachmentacrosscultures.org/research/.

Rogoff, B., Moore, L., Najafi, B., Dexter, A., Correa-Chavez, M. and Solis, J.

(2007) 'Children's development of cultural repertoires through participation in everyday routines and practices', in J.E. Grusec and P.D. Hastings (eds), *Handbook of Socialisation: Theory and Research*. New York: The Guilford Press. pp. 490–515.

Schweinhart. L.J., Montie, J., Xiang, Z., Barnett, W.S., Belfield, C.R. and Nores, M. (2005) *Finding of the Perry Preschool Programme Through to Age 40*. Ypsilanti, MI: HighScope Press.

Sims, M. and Hutchins, T. (1999) 'Positive transitions', *Australian Journal of Early Childhood*, 24(3): 12–16.

Siraj-Blatchford, I. (2004) 'Quality teaching in the early years', in A. Anning, J. Cullen and M. Fleer (eds), *Early Childhood Studies*. London: Paul Chapman Publishing.

Sylva, K., Melhuish, E., Sammons, P., Siraj-Blatchford, I. and Taggart, B. (2010) *Early Childhood Matters: Evidence from the Effective Pre-school and Primary Education Project*. London: Routledge.

Whalley, M. and the Pen Green Team (2007) *Involving Parents in their Children's Learning*. London: Paul Chapman Publishing.

Wylie, C. and Thompson, J. (2003) 'The long-term contribution of early childhood education to children's performance – evidence from New Zealand', *International Journal of Early Years Education*, 11(1): 69–78.

Index

Index

978-1-4462-0766-6

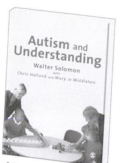

978-1-4462-0924-0

978-1-4462-1109-0

978-1-4462-0708-6

978-0-85702-535-7

978-1-4462-6719-6

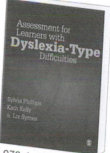

978-1-4462-6023-4

Find out more about these titles and our wide range of books for education practitioners at **www.sagepub.co.uk/education**

EXCITING SPECIAL EDUCATION NEEDS BOOKS FROM SAGE

The Behaviour Management Toolkit

Avoiding Exclusion at School

A Lucky Duck Book

Chris Parry-Mitchell

978-1-4462-1075-8

DAVE VIZARD

HOW TO MANAGE BEHAVIOUR IN FURTHER EDUCATION

AGE RANGE 16+

RESOURCES

2ND EDITION

978-1-4462-0283-8

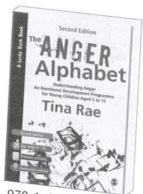

Second Edition

The ANGER Alphabet

A Lucky Duck Book

Understanding Anger
An Emotional Development Programme
for Young Children Aged 5 to 12

Tina Rae

978-1-4462-4913-0

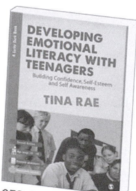

DEVELOPING EMOTIONAL LITERACY WITH TEENAGERS

A Lucky Duck Book

Building Confidence, Self-Esteem
and Self Awareness

TINA RAE

978-1-4462-4915-4

Bill Rogers

Third Edition

Classroom Behaviour

A Practical Guide to Effective Teaching, Behaviour
Management and Colleague Support

978-0-85702-167-0

Find out more about these titles and our wide range of books for education practitioners at **www.sagepub.co.uk/education**

EXCITING TITLES ON BEHAVIOUR MANAGEMENT FROM SAGE